STRAIGHT FROM THE SHOULDER

STRAIGHT FROM THE SHOULDER

'Throwing'—its history and cure

IAN PEEBLES

Foreword by Sir Donald Bradman

THE CRICKETER

HUTCHINSON

HUTCHINSON & CO *(Publishers)* LTD
and THE CRICKETER LTD
178–202 Great Portland Street, London W1

London Melbourne Sydney
Auckland Bombay Toronto
Johannesburg New York

★

First published 1968

*This book has been set in Baskerville, printed in Great Britain
on Antique Wove paper by Anchor Press, and
bound by Wm. Brendon, both of Tiptree, Essex*

09 087210 x

CONTENTS

ILLUSTRATIONS

Foreword
SIR DONALD BRADMAN

It was at Manchester in 1930 that I first batted against Ian Peebles.

At that time I didn't know we were born in the same year— nor did I know where our paths would lead.

My mind was too preoccupied with the frustrating experience of meeting a slow googly bowler whose delivery presented a hazard I had not previously encountered in that I could not detect his googly from his leg-break.

This would have been bad enough had the perpetrator of my discomfort been a fellow Australian, or even an Englishman, but he was a Scot.

His clan wasn't supposed to know much about cricket, let alone excel at it.

Now after a lapse of thirty-seven years, an intervening period during which friendship and respect have been nurtured by time and experience, I find myself complimented in being asked to write a foreword to his book.

Ian's reputation of itself was sufficient for me to say yes to his request before I scanned the manuscript.

Having read it, I approach my task with added pleasure but extreme humility, for I doubt my capacity to do justice to the book.

I love Scotland and its people.

I did not marry a descendant of the renowned Menzies Clan

for this reason but the happening has strengthened the ties.

The Scots have always been renowned for a charm of their own and many a Scottish golf professional has endeared himself to Australian hearts.

But they have not been outstanding contributors per medium of the written word to sports which are primarily of English origin.

At least in the cricket world I feel Ian Peebles has set a new standard, for here is a book about a most delicate and controversial subject, handled in the fashion of a master diplomat.

This is the most penetrating analysis of 'throwing' and history relating thereto that I have read.

It is a great education to traverse his detailed summary of events coupled with delightful expressions whereby events are put in their right perspective with a written charm even excelling that conveyed verbally by his melodious and disarming voice.

Not for him a phrase such as 'throwers are a menace to cricket'. No such offensive dictum. Instead we read that 'the bowler of illegitimate action is the most elusive and by far the most dangerous offender against the laws and spirit of the game'. No compromise in that polite condemnation. But no offence.

The same with umpires where he refers to their 'tolerance in the interpretation of the law'. No accusation of failing to do their job. But nevertheless he has not shrunk in these words from being adamant as to his point of view.

There is the delightful expression which conjures up a vision of a personality. This short but revealing reference to Sir Pelham Warner: 'His evidence is inconclusive; perhaps restrained by an extremely warm and charitable nature', at once produced a vision of my debating with that gentle ambassador in the Long Room at Lord's the relative virtues of Lockwood and O'Reilly.

There is a touch of pathos in his description of the closing moments of Griffin's Test career.

What a wealth of meaning when he describes that young bowler's effort to achieve an action which will satisfy the court of judgment, only to discover 'this new found security had been achieved at some cost in pace and life'. This is descriptive matter *par excellence*.

So it is when speaking of Mold that Peebles makes a magnificent contribution in support of educating the young bowler— the field wherein I have consistently claimed our greatest hope of success must lie—with these words:

'Had he been tutored to keep his arm straight when young, he might still have been the great wicket-taker he was, without stigma.'

Humour there is in abundance, though I confess the examples may kindle my laughter more than most because of my intimate knowledge of the characters involved.

Who could avoid chuckling to himself, despite the serious side of it, at the reference to 'Dainty' Ironmonger having lost the first finger of his left hand down to the middle joint 'as a result of a naive curiosity in the workings of a circular saw'?

Is there anyone who saw Jimmy Burke bowl who couldn't visualise him in the act by the comparison with 'a constable laying his truncheon on a very short offender's head'?

And as one who was the victim of a handshake with Ernie Jones I can endorse unequivocally the wonderment of the Hon. F. S. Jackson as to whether the cracked rib which 'Jonah' gave him with a fast delivery, or the handshake of apology, was the more painful experience.

These touches of humour simply add colour to the seriousness and value of Peebles' work.

At no stage does he 'accuse' players with doubtful actions. He even excuses the excesses of which we know they are capable in front of patriotic crowds by such as this—'the weight of evidence is that in over-enthusiastic moments his action was not blameless'.

There is little doubt that every 'throwing' controversy has tended to get out of perspective because of the natural inclination for the patriots and for the press of one country refusing to condemn their own representatives in the heat of battle—a charge which could be fairly levelled at almost every cricketing country.

It reminds me of something I read in *The Life of Lord Birkett of Ulverston*. Birkett was appearing for the defence of some Italians and heard the prosecuting council declare: 'These aliens should not be allowed to carry loaded firearms.'

That inimitable mind, which still lives in my memory despite the passing of the body, quickly produced its retort.

'If my learned friend had been defending instead of prosecuting they would have been *"Our Glorious Allies"*.'

The virtue of patriotism seems to hang precariously according to which side you are on.

But don't let me spoil the reader's pleasure by overdoing quotations in this foreword.

Let me turn to what I should perhaps describe as the more serious side of this book.

Peebles enlightens everyone by detailing the vast amount of time and effort which legislators have put into a study and attempted solution of the problem of doubtful bowling actions.

His findings, or perhaps I should say his disagreement with certain recommendations, may be construed in some quarters as a castigation of their efforts. But I do not think this would be in Peebles' mind.

Whilst not endorsing some legislative attempts, I am sure he is sympathetic with an underlying motive that at all costs an innocent man shall not be adjudged guilty.

It is in this field I find Peebles' conclusions so impressive.

The deep thought of a penetrative and analytical brain has come up with arguments so powerful and logical that any fair-minded and impartial reader will be hard-pressed to avoid agreeing with him.

It is incontestable that if his 'horizontal' law was used it would be impossible for a bowler to throw.

And it would be worth while for every legislator to think and think again on his hypothesis that if his theory affected adversely any existing bowlers their numbers would be few (if any), whereas the benefits of training future generations in such a fashion would bring incalculable benefits.

These are the thoughts of a truly impartial and independent observer.

His technical synopsis of what causes a doubtful action and how it can be rectified is first class and portrays the insight of a man who thoroughly understands the problem.

The latter is important. Too often we find in this sort of field that the stonemason is asked to adjudicate on a matter which can only reveal its secrets to a trained surgeon.

Even his reference to considering a penalty of ten runs or so to be debited against the bowler's own average for a 'called' delivery instead of the one extra at present added to sundries (with no penalty against the bowler) is more than intriguing—it is worthy of serious thought as a real deterrent.

Peebles' soft language must not be construed as compromise. For instance, when he says 'the particular law specifically states that doubt is sufficient ground for condemnation' he makes it crystal clear what he thinks and where the umpire's duty lies.

But it does not cause him to lose sight of the umpire's predicament. The great Birkett himself could scarcely have put the case better for those unfortunate people than this:

'The law says the umpire must speak up if not satisfied. But at what point does he become dissatisfied? In the knowledge that the result of his decision can well be the end of a career such as he himself has probably enjoyed the umpire may entertain doubts yet hesitate to declare that these amount to dissatisfaction. This may smack of moral cowardice but umpires are human and engaged in a very humane occupation.'

It is his discernment and appreciation of every angle of this vexed and difficult question which makes Peebles' analysis so valuable as well as readable.

Finally we should all be grateful for the historical search

B

which has brought forth the information contained in the Appendix.

As the fortunate possessor of the necessary copies of *Wisden* I was lucky enough to have read much of this information before.

But no such ready access is available to the great majority of cricket lovers, who will be grateful and fascinated by this peep into history and, might I say it, should be regarded as more than appendix information. The evidence therein must surely have a tremendous impact on the thinking of anyone who, officially or unofficially, aspires to contribute towards a solving of the problem.

In the modern era we so often come across books designed to cash in on the alluring publicity attached to some sensational event. Regrettably the pseudo work of a ghost lurking in the shadows of a famous name for monetary reward is all too obvious.

Every line of Peebles' splendid book carries the imprint and personality of the author.

As one who has lived through much of the period under review and who has not been a stranger to the administrative and selectorial problems involved, I express my gratitude to Ian for a splendid contribution to cricket history.

It is a treatise of great sincerity and charm. His arguments are powerful and must surely be respected even by those who cannot bring themselves to share his theories, but whose numbers will surely diminish on reading them.

Adelaide
September 1967

Introduction

As far back as the accurate history of the game can reach, the length of a cricket pitch has been twenty-two yards. Presumably early trial and error established the fact that a distance somewhere in this region between bowler and batsman was the most convenient for both to practise his skills, and constituted a fair balance between the two. That the exact figure was standardised at twenty-two yards was no doubt due to the fact that the chain was an everyday measure, used by anyone connected with the measurement of land.

When the length of the pitch was decided upon the element of safety could scarcely have been a major consideration, for the bowling was still the underhand trundling of the ball all along the ground. Since that point bowling has gone forward by three clearly definable stages. First came the introduction of 'length' bowling, which enormously enhanced the scope of both batsman and bowler. There followed, not without considerable opposition, the round-arm school, again with its profound influence on the techniques of the game. From there the raising of the arm to full overhand was a logical and almost inevitable step, although this also met with strong resistance from the more conservative elements.

When one considers the gap between the powers of Lindwall and 'Lumpy' Stevens it is an astonishing reflection that the length of the pitch has, without alteration, proved equally fair and satisfactory in both cases. There have, of course, been many safeguards and developments to ensure that the balance of power and safety has been maintained between the contesting parties.

The full power of Lindwall released against the Men of Hambledon, naked and unpadded, on a contemporary Broad-halfpenny pitch, would not only have been unplayable, but dangerous to a degree unnerving even to such a tough, stout-hearted generation.

His contemporaries found Lindwall a sufficient handful on the most perfect pitches that years of experience could provide, and their persons fairly adequately protected by box, pads and gloves. When such pitches were rendered uncertain by rain, or wear and tear, only the most skilled batsman could offer effective resistance. In all circumstances only the very skilled are equipped to defend themselves against the really fast bowler should he, accidentally or purposefully, seek to frighten or actually strike them with the short bouncer. Thus it is a convention, so strong as to be an unwritten law, that fast bowlers do not ever attack the helpless. I can only recall this moral code being broken on one occasion.

These points I cite in support of a fairly obvious fact. It is that the balance between batsman and bowler, basically established by the unvarying length of the pitch, has remained an almost perfect one but, as such, extremely delicate. Innovations and, occasionally, mistakes have demonstrated how readily it can be upset on either side.

A match played at Chesterfield in 1946 provided a good example of this delicacy and vulnerability. That highly efficient Yorkshire opening pair Bowes and Smailes had a very discouraging spell against the early Derbyshire batsmen, lacking both pace and length. The game had been in progress for some time when Len Hutton, who had been watching with growing suspicion from third man, voiced the view that the pitch was too long. A re-measurement confirmed that this was indeed so by a matter of two yards.

On the other side, any advantage afforded the bowler can have an equally decisive effect. In the ordinary way this comes from deterioration in the pitch from age or weather, abnormal morning dews or helpful breezes and fairly exploited are an essential and stimulating element in the game. The batsman defeated by legitimate means ought to have no complaint, nor ought he to be in any danger of serious injury.

The cricketer who, albeit unintentionally, gains advantage by infringing the laws introduces an entirely different element. There have been innumerable instances of sharp practice in the history of cricket, mostly trivial and usually laughable, to be grouped under the tolerant heading of 'gamesmanship'. When these have been mechanical rather than psychological one regrets to say that the bowler has been the more frequent culprit, for, as the prime mover, his opportunities have been the greater. Resin or eucalyptus on a handkerchief, to give more grip, raising the seam, polishing the ball and suchlike, have been hunted down over the years, but the writer has an unconcealed sympathy for such gentle aids, for no petty restrictions are put upon the batsman in the maintenance of his implements.

Perhaps because of this no batsman has been guilty of any flagrant violation of the moral code since 'Shock' White had his 'jumbo size' bat chopped down to respectable dimensions by the Hambledonians. True, W.G.'s bat once failed to satisfy the gauge, but this mishap would not have arisen had he not been a trifle hasty in suspecting that of the rival captain, and so invited retaliation.

Over recent years there has been recrudescence of the most elusive and by far the most dangerous offender against the laws and spirit of cricket in the shape of the thrower, or bowler of illegitimate action. It is not a new problem, but in the modern context it is an infinitely more difficult one to solve than when last it reached sufficient proportions to call for official action. Seventy years ago, in a more autocratic age, it could be summarily eradicated without reference to a number of independent cricketing powers with different and conflicting views, and authority, especially in the person of Lord Harris, was not likely to be questioned.

In this more sophisticated, and possibly more enlightened, generation there are a great many controversial voices raised on the subject, but they are raised because most are agreed upon one basic fact. It is that the thrower is thoroughly bad for the game, morally wrong and a potent source of physical danger. That the offender in most cases is honest of motive and convinced of his own orthodoxy would also be accepted by the objectors, but this concession merely increases their difficulties.

In this book I have endeavoured to put the problem in some perspective against the whole history of the malaise. It is also written to present a case for what I have long considered to be the most effective means of combating the evil. This is basically at variance with the official policy as formulated by the then Imperial Cricket Conference and, on the domestic scene, by M.C.C. and the 'throwing' committee set up in 1965. The members of these bodies are almost all practical cricketers of great experience, and their findings must be received with great respect by all responsible people. It is my contention, however, that in their efforts to be just, or perhaps generous, to all parties they have landed themselves so much unnecessary complication that they have 'scotched the snake, not killed it'. Admittedly, the ideas I have put forward over the years are untried and the 'horizontal law' is still in the realm of theory. Only practical trial could determine whether it would be as practical (and economical) as I would expect. My own observations and experiments lead me to believe that it would, but it is left to the reader to judge whether I have made sufficient case for serious official experiment.

In making research into the subject many interesting sidelights have come to view. I was much astonished to learn that so great a thinker and exponent of the art of bowling as F. R. Spofforth at one time advocated the legalising of throwing. It was interesting to learn that had not Alletson achieved fame through his hurricane innings at Hove he would probably have had to be content with a small degree of notoriety as a rather obscure bowler of doubtful action.

Those who at one time or another have been 'called' for throwing make an interesting cross-section of the cricket world in themselves. There are, at random, the scholarly C. B. Fry, two aborigines, a gallant soldier baronet killed in action at the beginning of the First World War, and a man who, despite his illegal action, failed to get a wicket in a career of four years with his county. So far as one can ascertain their status, amateurs and professionals seem to be equally represented.

As the instances quoted are confined to first-class cricket I have not found room in the text to mention the two favourite transgressors within my own experience. The first I encountered long years ago in the Highlands where there was a 'chucker' of commanding presence and considerable skill. The umpire when challenged by a disgruntled visiting batsman laughed the matter off with what he obviously regarded as a final and adequate explanation. 'Naw, naw', he said. 'He worrks in the slaughter hoose—and he got his action slittin' sheep.'

The other was an amusing schoolmaster named Heniker-Gottley, who was a self-confessed 'thrower', being for some reason unable to bowl. This came to light at the Faulkner School of Cricket, where, however, his very slow, innocuous throws were found to be ideal for the coaching of small boys. He recalled that of recent years he had only had one opportunity to practise his art in the middle, at East Molesey, on the banks of the Thames, when owing to a transport muddle only four of his side were present when play was due to start. A start was made regardless with seven substitutes, and he was deputed to throw, unfortunately, from the Thames end. To the chagrin of the batsmen he was stopped after his second over, not by the umpire, but on the intervention of the home club. When seven balls had been struck into the river, the secretary emerged and courteously explained that the spaniel trained to retrieve them, although more than equal to normal duty, was now exhausted, and the club's resources were nearing the same state.

This book makes no bones about being controversial. It would scarcely serve its purpose were it not, for opinion upon its subject is sharply divided.

There is one point which should be clearly underlined. It does not impugn the personal reputation or question the honesty of purpose of any one of the various bowlers involved in this controversy. For one very good reason it would be quite illogical to do so. Surely the essence of sharp practice of cheating is the *covert* and deliberate disregard or breaking of a rule or agreement. The suspect bowler subjects himself to the judgment of the umpires and up to eighty thousand people. He makes no attempt to conceal anything, in the confidence that, in his own judgment, he is in no way infringing the letter or the spirit of the law. Whether or not the bowlers in question have *infringed* the law remains a matter of honest opinion. Their reasons if they have done so are no more culpable than those who used to 'drag', another nebulous situation clearly resolved by the introduction of the front-foot law. Until this innovation many bowlers were suspect of infringement but no one suggested the advantage gained was deliberate or a cheat. The cases are further parallel in that the umpires, in the absence of clear guidance, were at some variance in their interpretations.

What I have sought to do is to clarify the situation, I would hope to the point where there could be no doubt whatsoever. If this can be achieved the problem would never arise as bowlers would be trained to the required standard from the very start in early youth.

I am most grateful to Mr. Norman Preston, the editor of *Wisden*, for his generous help. Also to the authors and publishers of the various books I have consulted. Particularly I am indebted to Mr. Irving Rosenwater for much help in providing material, correcting proofs, and for his general and unstinting co-operation.

The Dog it was that Died

A TRAGIC TRIO

G. M. GRIFFIN

In the later days of June 1960 England played the second Test match of the series against South Africa at Lord's. Although his side lost the match by an innings, it was a great occasion for young Geoffrey Griffin. At the age of twenty-one he became the first South African to do a hat-trick in Test-match cricket. This he did by having Mike Smith caught at the wicket off the last ball of one over, and clean bowling P. M. Walker and Trueman with the first two of his next.

The performance had not been without blemish. There had been much adverse comment upon his action wherever he had been seen in England, but apologists attributed any irregularity to a slight malformation of his right arm due to a boyhood accident. In the eyes of many critics, however, this was insufficient explanation for a very pronounced bend in the delivery swing.

One of them was F. S. Lee, one-time opening batsman for Somerset, and now a highly respected and senior umpire of wide experience. In the South Africans' match against the M.C.C. in May, Lee, in company with another well-known cricketer turned umpire, John Langridge, had thrice called Griffin for throwing. This was without precedent, for no visiting cricketer in England had ever before been no-balled on account of his action. A week later when playing against Nottinghamshire Griffin was again called eight times by two different umpires, Copson and Bartley. With this weight of opinion against him Griffin, no doubt in consultation with his captain and manager, did a most sensible thing. He went to seek the aid of Alf Gover, a great authority on the technicalities of the bowling action.

Gover spent three days with Griffin on the Spencer Club ground at Wandsworth in a thorough investigation and an intensive cure. By dint of getting Griffin's left shoulder round, and generally converting Griffin to a more sideways delivery, Gover seemed to have eliminated the suspect element of the swing. On his return Griffin came through the Whitsun match at Cardiff unscathed, and was picked for the first Test match at Edgbaston. Here again neither umpire found fault, but it seemed that this new-found security had been achieved at some cost in pace and life. It was probably in trying to regain this margin that Griffin again struck trouble, which he did in the following match at Southampton. Against Hampshire he was called six times, jointly by Parks and Harry Elliott.

For the Lord's Test match Lee had as his partner Syd Buller, a Yorkshireman who had emigrated to Worcester in his playing days, and was recognised not only as a top-class umpire but also as a man who was fearless in the discharge of his duties.

It so happened that Griffin bowled all of his thirty overs from the pavilion end during England's only innings so that, so far as the legality of his action was concerned, he was chiefly subject to Lee's jurisdiction. It was clear that he caused the umpire a good deal of hard thought throughout the innings, and sufficient doubt to be called on no less than eleven occasions. It is probable that even these dark portents did little to mar the young man's glorious moment, and life must have seemed full of joy when he returned to a great ovation, a record holder, and his side's most successful bowler. When one has reached one's twenty-first birthday but twelve days previously it is difficult to imagine that such prosperity is not certain for such time as seems a permanency.

The South African batting was scarcely so successful.

Statham twice ran through the side, ending with eleven wickets for 97 runs to give England victory by an innings and 73 runs. As the match was all over by 2.25 on the fourth day, it was arranged to play an exhibition match which the public were promised in the event of an unduly early finish to the main event.

These exhibition matches were light-hearted affairs in which spectators found some diversion, but which the players, not unnaturally, found rather irksome. This particular occasion could hardly be described as light-hearted.

Griffin again bowled from the pavilion end, so that this time he was observed by Buller from the square-leg position. Immediately Buller's voice was raised, and everyone present must have realised that for Griffin it was the voice of doom. Of his first five balls Buller rejected four, and the scene was more painful because it was obvious that Griffin was wholly unable to accommodate his action, even to the extent of getting through this one dismal over. It seemed that the trial might be unending, but at this point Jackie McGlew mercifully intervened, advising Griffin to finish the over underhand, with which advice Griffin immediately complied. Even so, his humiliation was not completed, for, omitting to warn the batsman of the change, he was promptly no-balled by Lee at the bowler's end. The over was then completed and Griffin retired to bowl no more for South Africa.

This was the saddest moment I have ever experienced in cricket, recalling half a century's association with the game. The most insensitive person present must have shared the general depression which followed this scene, which knocked all pretence of fun or entertainment out of the so-called exhibition match. The crowd collectively was far from insensitive, and strove to express its sympathy by applauding Griffin extravagantly whenever he fielded the ball, or gave them any excuse to do so. It was also noticeable that, in other places, whenever Griffin appeared in any role, the British public went out of its way to welcome him, and clearly wished it to be seen that they regarded him as a hapless victim rather than offender. This was warming and kindly but, if anything, only underlined the tragedy which had befallen a fine young cricketer.

In writing this book I have sought to make one particular point which this scene seems to epitomise, and which does not seem to have been widely appreciated. It may be flippantly but accurately expressed as 'pity the poor chucker'. For whilst the chucker causes resentment, confusion and occasionally physical danger, albeit without evil intention, it is he himself who ultimately is the chief sufferer.

*   *   *

A. MOLD

The case of Arthur Mold had a much greater impact on the cricket world of his day than that of Griffin sixty years later. Except that both ended sadly, his story differs in almost every respect.

Arthur Mold was a Northamptonshire man, born in 1865, at Middleton Cheney, near Banbury. His native county was not, in the days of his early manhood, a first-class county, and Mold soon started to cast about for a more suitable stage for his conspicuous talents. This he found in Lancashire, whence he emigrated and qualified, in time to play in the season of 1889. For Lancashire his arrival was welcome and timely, for they had just lost the services of Crossland, whose action had long been the subject of complaint, and which had eventually provoked Lord Harris into a decisive campaign which had in fact, if not technically, ended Crossland's career.

Mold was an immediate success. In his first season he took a hundred wickets, an achievement which became a habit thenceforward. In 1893 he was the leading fast bowler in England and, except for Lockwood, the only one of the highest class, when chosen to play against Australia in the three Test matches of that year. But as his career flourished, so the murmurings against his action increased. As in the case of his predecessor, opinion was divided. The Lancastrians rather naturally once again sprang to the defence of a colleague. W.G. was quoted as saying that Mold was 'the fairest of bowlers', a forthright verdict that must have deterred a number of accusers. The majority of his opponents thought rather differently, and Sydney Pardon, the editor of *Wisden*, was implacable in his opposition. Once again no one was absolutely certain as to what, and at what point, contravened law.

Pictures of Mold at this time show a finely built, handsome man, who might well have been taken as a model for the British Grenadier. He was also a man of extremely pleasant nature and manners. In after years Sir Pelham Warner recalls that he was deprived of some weeks of the season of 1900 by a blow on the leg from Mold, and goes on to describe his assailant:

'Many people thought that Mold's action was not above suspicion, but personally I think it would be difficult to say that he actually threw. If one watched him from the ring, sideways, one thought his action fair; but at the wicket one would swear that he occasionally threw a ball. . . .

'Mold was a beautiful bowler to watch. Three or four steps up to the wicket, a beautiful body swing, and the ball was propelled at a great pace. His off-break used to nip off the ground with lightning speed. . . . Personally, Mold was the nicest of men, and I am certain that he never intentionally threw.'

In the last sentence lie the undertones of tragedy. The technical evaluation is less convincing. Almost every chucker looks fair from side view at a distance, for few human eyes can follow the exact path of the hand and at the critical moment the bend of the arm is concealed by the fact that, to the spectator so positioned, the arm is in line from shoulder to viewpoint. Perhaps the point is clearer if one likens this view to looking at a wheel end on, when the curve is not apparent. Sir Pelham's assessment from the crease is much more germane, for, of all places, this is the most advantageous position. There was never a greater lover of cricket than 'Plum' and, a modern generation please note, never one who had a greater appetite and mastery in the realm of research, be it technicalities, tactics or personalities, down to minute detail. His evidence is inconclusive, perhaps restrained by an extremely warm and charitable nature, but this particular law specifically states that doubt is sufficient grounds for condemnation.

By the turn of the century Mold was still in his best form, having lasted a dozen strenuous seasons by dint of splendid physique and economical method. The first year of the new century brought the first portent of disaster. On Monday the 25th of June 1900 the match between Lancs and Notts began at Trent Bridge, and Mold came under the eagle eye of Jim Phillips, an Australian who divided his umpiring duties between this country and that of his birth. He had already achieved a reputation for dauntless courage and commendable indifference to the raucous clamour aroused by his views in some quarters. He had no-balled the great Ernest Jones in Australia for throwing, which must have been a fair test of nerve in itself.

The wicket at Nottingham was on the soft side, so for once Mold did not lead the attack. When he appeared as first change Phillips promptly no-balled him thrice in his first over. The Lancashire captain, A. C. MacLaren, recognising that here could be no compromise, took Mold off, and he bowled no more in the match. Phillips' action had far-reaching results, but one rather lesser one was that it broke Mold's long sequence of 100 wickets a season, for he had to be content in this summer with but 97.

In the winter of that year the county captains met and thoroughly endorsed Phillips' judgment by voting, by a majority of eleven to one, that Mold was an unfair bowler. Sydney Pardon was equally convinced of its justice, saying in forthright words that Mold was a lucky man to have survived the previous seasons without intervention.

It was in July of 1901 that Somerset won the toss and batted first at Old Trafford with, once again, Phillips on guard. His doubts were soon re-aroused and, by the end of the Somerset innings of 253, Mold had been no-balled sixteen times, in each case for illegal delivery. The sensation was, at least in sporting circles, nation-wide. It was also to all intents and purposes the end of Mold's cricketing days. Remembering Sir Pelham Warner's words one can say it had been an honourable career, if an unfortunate one. Its melancholy epitaph was supplied by Mold himself, who said he wished he had been stopped at the beginning of his career, for what had happened discredited all his great performances. Perhaps he would, in his honesty, have been more accurate to say that had he been tutored to keep his arm straight when young he might still have been the great wicket-taker he was, without stigma. It would in all probability have been off a longer run.

*　　*　　*

I. MECKIFF

Ian Meckiff first sailed into the ken of British cricketers when he toured with the Australian side in South Africa in 1957–8. The great era of Lindwall and Miller-cum-Johnston had just about come to an end and, despite occasional eruptions from the volcanic Miller, and the superb left-handed pace of Davidson, there was an obvious vacuum to be filled (at the expense of a good muddled metaphor) by a likely lad. It seemed that Meckiff was the man and his record on the series of eleven wickets at 32 apiece, if not brilliant, was a basis for further consideration. There was but one serious objection. Rumours filtrated to this country that his action was somewhat peculiar and, if not modified, might lead to controversy. One particular rumour was to the effect that, although his hosts were convinced that he was suspect, there had been a tacit agreement amongst umpires that none would raise what was bound to be an unpleasant issue. If true, this charitable gesture, as many of a like nature, was to lay up a packet of trouble for the future.

Later in this book I have gone into the controversies which arose on the 1958–9 M.C.C. tour of Australia in some detail in tracing the history of throwing in general. In studying the effect of these stories on the man himself it is well to try to see the situation from his point of view.

In 1960, when feeling still ran high, Meckiff, in collaboration with a professional journalist, published a book entitled *Thrown Out*. In his preface Meckiff passionately defends his good name as a fair bowler and in block capitals protests 'I DO NOT THROW'. The sincerity of this statement is unquestioned, but the author, and his confidant, are rather less generous towards the views of the visiting press.

According to the book there was no disapproval of Meckiff's action until his spectacular success at Melbourne in the second Test match in England's second innings. This was just not true. Despite the doubts voiced in South Africa all those who had not seen Meckiff bowl approached the question with open mind. After the State match against Victoria there was no one in the visiting party without grave doubts, and a large faction who said in forthright terms that Meckiff was a chucker. From the distance and angle of the press box it was not so easy to be certain, but the players were quite certain that this was not bowling. What seemed possible, in light of Meckiff's limited success in the match, was that the matter might be brushed off without major incident. But when Meckiff was picked for the first Test match at Brisbane a violent collision became almost inevitable. The situation was exacerbated by the fact that, after England's poor showing, any criticism of Meckiff was bound to be interpreted as a 'squeal' by those who saw nothing amiss with his action. May and the M.C.C. management held their peace, and all parties arrived at Melbourne in a state of mounting tension.

In England's second innings Meckiff cut loose, and there was at least no doubt as to his power of destruction. In 15.2 overs he took six wickets for 38 and decided the issue of the match. It is true to say that this was the start of the controversy as an open and public breach.

Johnny Wardle had himself been a bitterly controversial figure. A quarrel with Yorkshire had led to a further difference with the M.C.C. and, instead of travelling as a member of the team, which could have made good use of his talents as a spinner, he had accepted a press assignment. On the evening of Meckiff's success the *Melbourne Herald* carried a front-page article, under banner headlines, in which Wardle denounced Meckiff in unrestrained terms.

The dispute was now wide open, and those who had previously held their fire now let fly. The reaction was, not unexpectedly, equally violent. The Australian press rose in defence of their team, and lambasted their opponents as 'squealers' and unsporting losers. In the heat of battle the grievances, resentfully nursed for over a year about the supposed rigging of the English Test wickets, flared up again with charge and countercharge whistling over the cables to London and back again. The more extreme Australian attitude was voiced by Jim Mathers, a somewhat excitable veteran, who wrote a powerful 'open letter' to the British press in which the King's English inadvertently came off rather worse than the offending journalists. So the quarrel continued in rising key and the series ended with no lessening of tension between the opposing camps.

It is clear from Meckiff's book that he considered himself the innocent victim of a malicious persecution on the part of the British press. Despite his innocence he considered it prudent to modify his action. The reason for this he sets out as follows. 'I decided to make this change before I went on the 1959–60 tour of India and Pakistan. The Indians were to visit England after the 1958–9 tour of Australia and they no doubt would have seen reports that I was a chucker. They were also invited to see films of Rorke, Slater and myself bowling, so I thought, where there's fuel there's fire and decided to keep my arm straight right from the word go so that it would look as if my arm was perfectly straight throughout my whole bowling action.'

It is difficult to see how this alteration could be at all effective unless he maintained this straightness during the final arc, from the horizontal to the point of delivery, for this was the area in which his action had always been a subject of comment. Pro-

C

vided a bowler is extended during this section of his swing it is impossible for him to throw, however he may bend or flex in preparation. Observers who flew out to watch the Australian series against the West Indies in the season of 1960–1 thought that Meckiff had succeeded in ironing out the kink in the final swing and, in consequence, was orthodox but ineffective. Meckiff maintains with considerable force that his loss of form was due to injury, and states that the conspirators deliberately ignored this fact. In two Test matches against the West Indies he took two wickets for 234, a record which leaves room for both schools of thought.

It was about this time that Sir Hubert Ashton, as President of M.C.C., held a press conference to discuss the decisions of the Anglo-Australian meeting regarding the forthcoming Australian tour of England. The opening words of Meckiff's book read: ' "10 feet tall, bowls at 3,000 miles an hour, and tries to kill batsmen." ' According to a reporter on the *Melbourne Herald*'s staff, that's the impression he got when he listened to thirty top English cricket writers quizzing M.C.C. President, Sir Hubert Ashton, in November 1960. To one who was also present (and incidentally slightly misquoted in the book) this is a weird impression, and an uncertain note upon which to open a controversial book. My recollection is of a gathering, sober and anxious for the success of the proposed truce, but scarcely optimistic. One point was abundantly clear. If the British journalists considered the throwing controversy a good story, as did Meckiff and his colleague, they were entirely sincere in their charges, and genuinely concerned about the damage it was doing to the game of cricket, and to elements beyond it.

Meanwhile Meckiff, presumably persevering with his new action, was bowling for Victoria with modest success. In the successive seasons of 1960–1 and 1961–2 he averaged 27 in Sheffield Shield cricket. 1962–3 brought an improvement to an average of 19. In that season he played against the M.C.C. team in both matches for Victoria with fair success, but did not appear in any of the Test matches.

The next season brought the South Africans to tour in Australia and an early resurgence of Meckiff's fortunes. Topping the Sheffield Shield averages with eleven wickets at 19 apiece he was selected for the first Test match which started at Brisbane on the 6th of December. Australia batted into the second day to make 435 and when they took the field McKenzie bowled the first and uneventful over. Umpire Egar saw this through and retired to square-leg to watch Meckiff deliver the second over of the innings. The first ball went unchecked but, on the second, Egar shouted 'No-ball'. The third he called, then the fifth, and the ninth. In those few minutes Egar ended Meckiff's career. He also demonstrated that the British press had not been insincere in their objections and, quite clearly, that Australia had finally and decisively put her house in order. For his pains Egar was roundly booed by one section of the crowd.

This official confirmation of their long-held views was gratifying to the parties concerned, but for the main actor it was tragedy. The moment of restoration and the prospect of a return to the glory of an all Australian opening bowler were abruptly dashed. How heavy had been the fall from 'ten feet tall'. At the interval he was carried shoulder high from the field, an irony which must have underlined the disappointment of the day. He bowled no more in the match, and presently announced his retirement from cricket.

Some say that finding little prospect of success with his new action he had decided to revert to his original delivery, and put it to the crucial and final test. One rather hopes that this is so, for, if true, he would have been prepared for a final verdict one way or another.

So, after a career which had evoked much bitterness, departed a very agreeable and personally popular young man. I am convinced of his honesty of purpose, as perhaps he now is of the honesty of his critics. But nothing will ever convince me that the verdict was unjust.

History

In 1833 John Nyren published his *Young Cricketer's Tutor*. He
was then in his sixty-ninth year, living in Bromley, Middlesex.
His love for cricket was as great as ever and he was a lively
observer and critic of the contemporary scene.

It is a beautiful little book, written in a straightforward
practical style which reflects the robust honesty and common
sense of the author. It is dedicated to William Ward, whose
combined abilities as a banker and a cricketer did so much for
cricket in general and saved Lord's cricket ground from being
built upon at an early stage in its history. The dedication is
worthy of the book, almost Johnsonian in its grave, dignified
courtesy, without trace of subservience.

It is the last paragraph of the dedication which immediately
concerns the subject of this book. In it Nyren exhorts his patron:
'. . . May you never relax your endeavours to restore the game
to the good old principles from which, I regret to say, it has in
some instances departed since I was a member of the fraternity.
You are aware that I principally allude to the practice that the
modern bowlers have introduced of throwing the ball, although
in direct infringement of a law prohibiting that action.'

Having made his point Nyren then proceeds to the instruc-
tional part of the book, guiding the novice through such intrica-
cies as a ball inside the leg stump shooting along the ground,
but, before embarking on his reminiscences of Hambledon, he

returns to his original charge with a manifesto headed:
'PROTEST—against the modern innovation of throwing
instead of bowling the balls.' It makes interesting and pertinent
reading to modern eyes and is quoted in full in the Appendix
to this book.

The evil which excited Nyren's indignation was the same in
principle as the problem which has arisen periodically in the
last eighty years, and is still recurrent—that is to say, the bowler
whose methods infringe the spirit and, so far as it has been
defined, the letter of the law, thus gaining an unfair advantage.
As in Nyren's day all the bowling was underhand, the technicalities were very different, and what he describes as throwing
(in relation to bowling) would now be quite legitimate. His
concern was with the raising of the arm to anything up to
shoulder height, or what was later legalised as round-arm
bowling. Provided the arm was respectably below the required
level he seems to have accepted any movement whether
straight or bent armed. Thus he describes in terms of admira-
tion the bowling of David Harris: 'His mode of delivering the
ball was very singular. He would bring it up from under the
arm by a twist, and by this action push it, as it were, away
from him.'

The first experimenter with the raised arm was Walker, a
prominent member of the Hambledon Club who had earlier
pioneered the slow, lobbing style of bowling. Influential members of the club immediately took action, and Walker's second
innovation seems to have been short-lived. Even so, it planted a
seed which was to sprout trouble or progress, according to the
observer's standpoint. It came to full flower in the early years
of the next century when John Willes of Kent proved a very
much more determined pioneer. His first whole-hearted
assault, metaphorically on the old order and physically upon
the contemporary batsmen, took place in 1807 at Penenden
Heath. It must have been a crowded as well as a controversial
scene, for he was playing for no less than Twenty-Three of
Kent against Thirteen of England. His new-fangled style

caused a good deal of resentment, and was described by the press of the day as 'a great obstacle against getting runs'. But Willes was undeterred in the face of much discouragement, ranging from hard words to minor riots. One or two imitators, notably Ashby and Lambert, helped to spread the controversy, but it was not until 1822 that the practice became an issue with authority. In that year Willes appeared for Kent against the M.C.C. and was at once no-balled by Noah Mann, a strong umpire with a Hambledonian father. Willes' exit was rather more dramatic, for, in the picturesque words of Mr. H. S. Altham, he 'threw down the ball in disgust, rode away out of Lord's, and out of cricket history'. But he too had sown a seed.

James Lillywhite was prepared to defy authority, as well as risking hard words and possible brawls. The time had now arrived, however, when there was much wider sympathy with the innovators, and Sussex, being prominent in promoting the new style, played three experimental matches which were designed to prove its worthiness as well as its superiority. Their opponents were, each time, All England. The only match to be lost was the third, in which a certain Mr. Knight, playing for England, seized upon the opposition's chief weapon and slew them with it. Knight became a firm champion of the new round-arm bowling, and proved as good an advocate on paper. One point he made holds good to this day. 'To describe the new style as throwing is nonsense', he wrote. 'The straight arm is the very antithesis of a throw.'

In 1828 the M.C.C. sought to control the situation with a rather curiously worded amendment to the law which permitted the arm to be raised as high as the elbow. This was tacitly ignored by the rapidly increasing new school and in 1835 M.C.C. bowed to the trend and legalised round-arm bowling. But, as this was unduly limiting nature and natural inclination, there were soon a number of arms swinging happily above the prescribed shoulder-high tide-mark, to inaugurate a new phase of an old problem. The most effective of these was that of Edgar

Willsher, who played for Kent from the fifties. His powers were enhanced by his being left-handed with a natural break from the leg and being unfettered—to the extent that each side supplied its own umpire, there being no central pool.

In 1862 All England came to the Oval to play Surrey, and once again there was a dramatic but, eventually, salutary incident. Willsher was no-balled seven times in a row by John Lillywhite, at which all nine England professionals left the field. The game proceeded on the next day, when Lillywhite was replaced by a less exacting umpire; but the point had been made. M.C.C., once again eschewing the role of Canute, amended the law in 1864 to allow the bowler complete freedom —at least of elevation.

If authority thought that this generosity would lead to an era of uninterrupted peace its hopes were due for disappointment. It seemed that amongst bowlers there were always those who, given a liberal inch, would sneak a covert ell.

In a few years' time there were rumours of unsatisfactory interpretations of the new law. This was a more complicated malaise than had hitherto troubled the game, for in this case diagnosis was a great deal more difficult. The level of the arm was an easily observable matter, and seldom in dispute as a matter of fact. This new disagreement, as its forerunner, arose entirely through the tolerance, or otherwise, of the players and umpires in their interpretation of the law concerned. But the illegal action in the shape of the bowl-cum-throw was an elusive offence, upon which opinion was honestly if strongly divided.

The chief suspects were in the North. Crossland of Lancashire, the only fast bowler of quality in the country during the late seventies and early eighties, was suspect number one. He seems to have been a robust, unaffected personality, and is probably the true and original author of the triumphant cry of 'There goes your blankety pulpit' on the violent dismissal of a cricketing clergyman. It is also said of him that, occasionally before releasing his fastest ball, he would precede it with a very

obvious foot fault in order to distract the umpire's attention
from the villainy to come—it still being only within the power
of the umpire at his end to call him. His two supporting slow
bowlers, Nash and Watson, were also regarded as being rather
more than doubtful cases by many opposing players. Across the
border Yorkshire considered that they had found a splendid
prospect in a young fast bowler named Harrison, but his
methods caused consternation in other counties.

Despite the outspoken objections from many quarters, the
North was largely in solid support of those bowlers, whose
methods they regarded as perfectly fair. The Lancashire
captain, A. N. Hornby, a most honest man of great experience,
had complete confidence in the legality of his attack.

It took the commanding personality of Lord Harris, a man
with a stern regard for law and order, to rally the objectors.
Immediately after Kent had been defeated at Old Trafford in
1885 he wrote a letter to Lancashire cancelling the return
fixture at Tonbridge. He reminded the Lancashire authorities
that whilst the other counties had agreed in 1883 not to play
bowlers who were thought to be beyond the law that they, in
company with Sussex and Gloucestershire, had demurred. He
protested his personal friendship for A. N. Hornby, but firmly
voiced his objections to Nash and Crossland.

To this Lancashire made a spirited reply, pointing out that
both these bowlers had been selected by the M.C.C. in the
previous year to represent the North against the South. The
disagreement might have reached deadlock had not Crossland
been found wanting in another direction. For some years his
residential qualification for Lancashire (another matter upon
which his Lordship was sensitive and vigilant) had been
questioned. Further investigation revealed that he had broken
it by living in Nottingham for a period during 1884. This was
indefensible in law, and Crossland retired from the scene, leaving a considerable bitterness amongst his supporters, directed
against Kent in particular and the South in general.

These measures effectively scotched the evil for a few years,

The Final Arbiters. Four umpires who have, in different ways, figured prominently in the history of throwing. Mel McInnes—Colin Egar—James Phillips—J. S. Buller.

**The orthodox straight-arm swing, seen from front and
side.** The arm, starting straight, swings through with the
unforced and co-ordinated turn of the trunk and shoulders. Full
extension is easily maintained throughout.

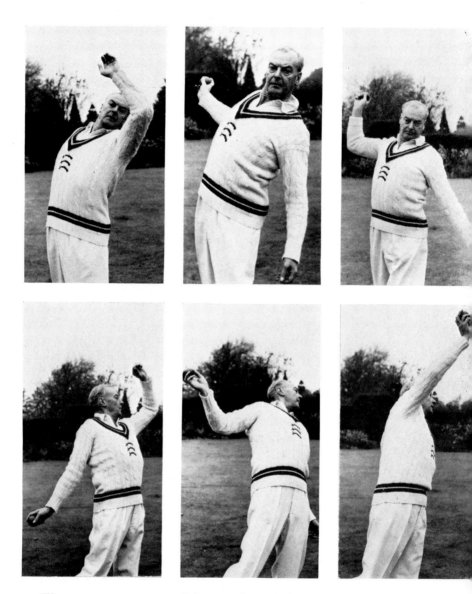

The premature turn of the trunk and shoulders, seen from the same positions. The chest is visible to the batsman whilst the arm is still well below the horizontal. It will be found on experiment that it cannot be swung through in a vertical plane from this position maintaining full extension. It is this premature turn of the trunk, resulting from a sudden extra effort on the part of the bowler, which compels him to bend and flex. See text, pages 55, 56

The perfect 'chucker's' action. Here is to be seen every characteristic of the bent-arm thrower. The turn of the chest, the arch of the back—and the splaying of the front foot in sympathy with the exaggerated twist of the trunk and shoulders. See text, pages 55, 58

but in the nineties it gradually reappeared. The Australians in the previous decade had been extremely outspoken about some of the suspects they had encountered on their trips to England. Now they found themselves confronted with the same problem within their own country.

Where suspect bowling was concerned, the two principals on the Australian scene were both South Australians, James Phillips and Ernest Jones, who in widely different ways made their own particular niches in cricket history.

Phillips qualified for Victoria and his talents as a medium-paced bowler, a fair batsman, and a smart cover-point earned him a place in the State side. He seems to have been restless to the point of wanderlust, for he then travelled to England and played for Middlesex in the nineties. Had he confined himself to the playing of the game his name would be long forgotten, but even before his active day was done he became an umpire. His impact on the game in this role was immediate, and very much greater than anything he had achieved as a player.

It is an interesting sidelight on Phillips' career that in 1899 he foreshadowed to some extent the efforts of future legislators to define a throw. Norman Preston, the present editor of *Wisden*, recounted in his notes for 1961 how he came across a booklet written in 1899 by Phillips. The passage quoted reads:

> I am one of those who hold the opinion that to bowl a fair ball it is immaterial whether the arm be straight or at an angle so long as there is no perceptible movement in the elbow-joint at the precise moment the ball leaves the hand of the bowler.
>
> Just as one bowler, in his desire to make his delivery more difficult, gets as near the return crease as possible, and occasionally inadvertently oversteps the mark, thereby bowling a 'no-ball', so another bowler will, in attempting an increase of pace, use his elbow, especially if he be a bowler whose arm is not quite straight. In each of these instances it does not seem just to suppose that either bowler is wilfully unfair.
>
> In my capacity as an umpire I have found that there is great

difficulty in detecting the elbow movement at the bowling end, whereas when standing at the batting end, near short-leg, this difficulty is overcome, and every movement of the bowler's arm is noticeable.

Ernest Jones was originally a miner of enormous physical strength. As this was combined with a fine elasticity, his fast bowling soon created awe and terror in rustic and suburban cricket in South Australia and in 1892 he started in the State side. In 1894–5 he played once for Australia, but, thereafter, was his country's official fast bowler until 1902. In 1896 he came to England and astonished his hosts with his pace. He also caused them a good deal of misgiving by his method of generating it.

Talking to *Wisden* in 1940 Sir Stanley Jackson recalled his early experiences with Jones. He opened the innings with W.G. for Lord Sheffield's team in 1896 when the Australians, fresh off the boat, were a bit short of practice. This seems to have affected Jones' accuracy rather than his pace, for the openers had a pretty rough time. This was the occasion when Jones got the ball near enough to W.G.'s chin to start the legend of the ball that went through his beard, for four byes. (My *Wisden* was inherited from a great student who points out in a marginal note that there were only two byes in the innings.) Sir Stanley denies that the ball actually penetrated that national emblem of British virility; but it caused W.G. to give it a hasty waggle out of harm's way. He does confirm 'Jonah's' immortal apology: 'Sorry, Doctor—she slipped.' Jackson also received a handsome apology from the same generous source. A thump on the ribs was later found to have cracked one of them and when next they met Jones endorsed his regrets with a handshake which left the recipient wondering which had been the more painful experience.

As a result of these incidents Harry Trott coached and advised Jones, and Sir Stanley says that off a shortened run he developed a beautiful action. Whatever his contemporaries may have thought, Jackson scouts the idea that Jones had a doubtful delivery, and puts him amongst the best fast bowlers that he had ever met.

Others were less sanguine. In 1897–8 Phillips returned to his native country with A. E. Stoddart's team as their official umpire. The opening State match was at Adelaide, and Phillips started his tour of office by calling Jones for throwing in front of his home crowd. It was a singularly courageous action, 'the incident', as *Wisden* says in its guarded way, 'naturally giving rise to a great deal of comment'. It does not seem to have affected Ranji, who made 189. Phillips, too, was undeterred and later called Jones in a Test match. But no other umpire took Phillips' view, or at any rate had the courage to voice it, so that Jones continued until his honourable retirement. This is a wholly pleasant reflection, for here again is the strangely recurrent theme of the generous good-hearted sportsman, wholly innocent of any evil intent, but suspect of what comes within the realm of sharp practice.

There is a glimpse of Jones in after years which, though trivial, has always pleased me. Gubby Allen met him at Adelaide in 1932 and told me that so impressive a figure did he make when in his sixties that he took a walk around him just to have a look. This, he said, with such a spread of shoulder and chest, was quite a stroll. Jones died in Adelaide in 1943, remembered as one of the great fast bowlers of all time and one whose name is linked with that of Kortright as the fastest ever. The weight of evidence is that in over-enthusiastic moments his action was not blameless.

The other prominent Australian transgressor was T. R. McKibbin, a spinner from New South Wales. In both his own country and in England his action was strongly questioned, especially when he bowled his off-break, a ball susceptible to the bent elbow. McKibbin was a deadly performer on occasions but inclined to be erratic, the characteristic of the big spinner which he certainly was, and the 'chucker' which he probably was.

In England the trouble was again comparatively rife. Of at least a dozen bowlers cited by opposing players as sinners the most important and controversial case came once again from Lancashire. Arthur Mold took over a hundred wickets in the season nine times during a career lasting from 1889 to 1901. He bowled very fast off a short run, with great life from the pitch and occasionally nipped back awkwardly from the off.

He played in the Test matches against Australia in 1893 and until the reign of Lockwood and Richardson was the leading fast bowler in England. He was a very different character from the flamboyant Crossland and whatever views players took of his bowling they entertained no personal animosity against the man. Looking back over a space of seventy years, and at the outcome of his career, Mold is a figure of tragedy, certainly not one of roguery.

There were amongst the other suspects some illustrious names, Kortright, Fry, and even Richardson being to the fore. The last-named is a strange inclusion to modern minds when one studies the splendid pictures taken of him by Beldam which give the clear impression of a beautiful straightforward swinging action, exactly in accord with the generous nature and physique of the man.

Many complained but no concerted action was taken during the nineties. Lord Harris was as ever outspoken, and Sydney Pardon, the editor of *Wisden*, campaigned with courage and vigour. The 'front line' fighter in this battle was again Jim Phillips, strong and fearless, now alternating between this country and his native Australia.

With the example of his strictures of Ernest Jones before them, urged by the strong climate of opinion and exhorted by Mr. Pardon, the English umpires began to take a firmer line. In 1898 C. B. Fry, for some years the subject of adverse comment, was no-balled on three separate occasions whilst playing for Sussex. He was called at Trent Bridge by West, and against Oxford University by Phillips. In July Sherwin no-balled him in the match against Middlesex at Lord's. F. J. Hopkins was called by Titchmarsh when bowling for Warwickshire against Kent at Tonbridge.

The following year saw three further cases. Captain E. R. Bradford played twice for Hampshire, against the Australians at Southampton and against Leicestershire in an away match. He batted with considerable success, but his fast bowling met with immediate disapproval. In the Australian match he was called by both umpires and at Leicester by Smith. In the same year H. Hardstaff made a solitary appearance for Notts, also against the Australians, and was called by West when he opened the bowling.

The season of 1900 was an eventful one. Fry was again called, this time by West in the Sussex match against Gloucestershire at Hove in his opening spell. This check seems to have had a salutary effect, for *Wisden* records that when he was tried for a second time his action was perfectly fair. The major event in the field of unfair bowling was Phillips' first action against Mold. At Trent Bridge he no-balled Mold in the first over he sent down, with such firm intention that Mold was retired at the end of it and bowled no more in the match. Later in the season Phillips no-balled E. J. Tyler, a very slow left-hander, whilst operating for Somerset against Surrey at Taunton. This instance was applauded by Pardon in his annual notes on the very reasonable grounds that it was a timely reminder that slow bowlers could be as guilty of transgression as their swifter colleagues.

The time had come for firm official support and in December 1900 the county captains met once more to decide what was to be done to keep their bowlers within the bounds of the law. Their suggestion to debar certain bowlers was overruled by the M.C.C. committee, but the threat of action had a salutary effect. In the next December, following a September meeting of the county captains, the M.C.C. addressed a letter to all county secretaries. Its content was, briefly, to the effect that no drastic measures were necessary, but a bowler disqualified on any particular occasion should not be re-employed in the match and that persistent cases should be banished for at least a season if condemned by a majority of two to one at a captains' meeting.

The Australian season of 1900–1 brought a further case to light. Crockett, a leading umpire in Sheffield Shield and Test-match cricket, no-balled J. J. Marsh twice in the New South Wales *v.* Victoria match at Melbourne, and no less than nineteen times in the return match at Sydney. Marsh was an aborigine and as a forerunner of Gilbert of later years one is tempted to speculate on the influence of the boomerang.

The year of 1901 was virtually the end of the 'throwing' epoch which had beset English cricket for the previous decade. At Manchester Phillips stood umpire in the Lancashire and Somerset match and this time mounted a full-scale attack upon Mold. In the first innings he judged sixteen balls from Mold to be illegal. This being done, he rested content and, although Mold bowled untrammelled in the second, it was his last appearance for his county. No other bowler was called during this English season, nor in 1902, but in 1903 Paish, the Gloucestershire slow bowler, was no-balled by West in successive matches against Nottinghamshire and Yorkshire, both at Bristol.

There followed a gap of five years' uninterrupted peace until 1908, when there arose a remarkable case. Once again the centre of the incident was a Lancastrian and Old Trafford the scene. Ralph Whitehead made his first appearance for his county against Nottinghamshire on June 29. When Lancashire batted, against a very goodish bowling side which included Hallam, Wass and Iremonger, he made a splendid 131 not out going in at number eight. Soon afterwards he had the galling experience of being called by T. Brown for throwing. The umpire was at pains to explain that it was only his faster ball to which he objected and, as Whitehead had no further trouble during his career with the county, it is reasonable to suppose that he hearkened to this warning.

Whitehead was the last case of a bowler being called for throwing in first-class cricket before the First World War. There were one or two bowlers who were not universally approved, but none officially checked. Some people looked a bit sidewise at Burns of Worcestershire, who worked up a great pace from time to time. It is also interesting to reflect that had not Alletson of Nottinghamshire gained fame and immortality in a tumultuous hour and a half at Hove when he smote Sussex for 189 he might have left no greater impression than the memory of a rather obscure county bowler of doubtful action.

The post-war period in England was almost entirely free of trouble in this direction and was, indeed, a period of beautiful actions on the part of both visitors and visited. The Australian side of 1921 relied on all important occasions on but four superb bowlers, all with model actions of their type. Gregory had the most rumbustious and awe-inspiring approach and delivery, but McDonald remains in the memory of all who saw him as the most graceful fast bowler in their experience. For a man of his immense bulk Armstrong had a remarkably neat, straight-arm action, ideally suited to his purpose, which was to drop his flighted top-spinners with consistent and mathematical accuracy. Arthur Mailey similarly had the perfect delivery for his particular stock-in-trade, which was an abundance of spin beyond any other tweaker.

Two years later the West Indies toured, bringing with them the beautiful bounding, wheeling actions of Francis and Constantine which came to be accepted as typical of the Caribbean bowler, and a most pleasing picture at that. One of their number, John, had, curiously enough, been called for throwing whilst playing against the M.C.C. touring side at Georgetown a dozen years previously, but no question concerning his action arose in this country. In South Africa cricket was still played exclusively on matting wickets and Nupen spun his fast-medium off-breaks with the full, free sling of the gymnast.

In England Tate and Larwood provided models of efficiency allied to functional beauty. Waddington of Yorkshire bowled fastish left-hand with a particularly pleasing delivery, and later his fellow Yorkshireman, Bill Bowes, made the maximum use of his great height with a high straight arm. At the other end of the scale so far as pace was concerned there were still fairly frequent glimpses of Wilfred Rhodes to demonstrate the virtues of simplicity and economy.

There were actions which attracted adverse attention but never to the extent of being no-balled. One of these was Alec Kennedy, of Hampshire, whose action was also remarkable for its perfect rhythm. His best ball was one which he cut from the leg and some thought that in doing so his arm bent and flexed. My own impression is that he was more inclined to shorten at the end of his swing as he snapped his wrist at the moment of delivery.

The same charge was made against George Geary, although not very seriously, in South Africa in 1927–8. Geary was a magnificent bowler on matting wickets, turning the ball both ways at a fast-medium pace with very little indication of his intentions to be read from his hand. After a most successful first Test match at Johannesburg, in which he took twelve wickets, he broke down in the second with a damaged elbow. Some of our opponents attributed this injury to the fact that he bent and jerked his arm in delivering his fast leg-cutter, which especially on the fast Johannesburg wicket was a deadly ball. Again I believe that there may have been the same final shortening of the swing, but the general effect was of a normal straight arm delivery.

Contemporaries in the Warwickshire side and opponents thought that at times N. E. Partridge threw his off-spinners and even more pronouncedly his faster ball. That he was never challenged may have been that the era was so generally free of throwing that it was never regarded as a serious problem and the general climate was one of benevolent tolerance.

But the most extraordinary suggestion to those who played with him in later years was made in *Wisden* of 1923 regarding G. O. Allen. It was said that he would have to exercise great care, especially in delivering his fastest ball. As one of those who did play a lot with Allen this is astonishing, for of all actions this one might well be taken not only as a model for any aspiring fast bowler but as a criterion for absolute orthodoxy and fairness.

In Australia there arose a somewhat unusual case of doubt. Bert Ironmonger was a stoutly built Victorian, reckoned to be the worst batsman and fielder ever to appear for his country. He was also in the opinion of Pat Hendren and other good judges the best slow-medium left-handed bowler of the day. He had lost the first finger of his left hand down to the middle joint (said to be the result of a naive curiosity in the workings of a circular saw) and he gripped the ball hard against the stump. In contrast to a general ungainliness, his run-up was so surprisingly light-footed that he was nicknamed 'Dainty', and he gave the ball such a tweak that it buzzed audibly on its flight, but a pronounced flexion of his left arm aroused outspoken criticism amongst visiting teams and certain doubts in Australian minds.

He never came to England, so I have to depend upon the testimony of those who played against him. One particular friend made quite a close study of the subject and watched him bowl all day through glasses. His verdict was definite. 'Before lunch', he said, 'he threw two balls in every over. Between lunch and tea he threw four an over. After tea, when he was tired, he threw the lot.'

When in Australia in after years I got to know Ironmonger quite well, and found him a genial companion and ready to talk freely about his action. He was quite emphatic that he was blameless, and laughingly said he was the victim of propaganda to keep him away from England. There was no doubt as to the honesty of his belief in his own orthodoxy. But this is by no means conclusive for, as I have maintained through this book, the 'chucker' is in most cases wholly honest of purpose.

R. Halcombe, of Western Australia, bowled very fast off a shortish run and came in for official disapproval. In the opinion of visiting English batsmen it was fully merited. The same batsmen in their own country had occasional qualms about Copson of Derbyshire, but these were mild and not universally supported. Some thought that Clarke of Northants

D

occasionally threw an extra quick one, and happening on a slow-motion newsreel shot, I must confess that I was much astonished. But as Mr. Tom Smith, the honorary general secretary of the Association of Cricket Umpires, wrote in *The Cricketer*: 'Action seen by the camera can be very misleading, especially in slow motion, when angles of perspective and fore-shortening give exaggeration.' That is very true and the author rightly says that it is essential to see the action 'live' in order to give a fair decision. It is a point I shall return to later.

There was no case of a bowler being 'called' in England in first-class cricket during the latter part of the thirties, and the last Australian case was that of H. J. Cotton of South Australia, who was no-balled at Melbourne in the season of 1936–7. With the arrival of the war attention was diverted in most cricket-playing countries to rather different missiles and their delivery and where cricket was played there was little newspaper space available in this country for its reporting. Thus the only recorded wartime case of throwing passed unnoticed, but Mr. Gerald Brodribb, in his most intriguing book of legal curiosities in cricket, *Next Man In*, cites a case in the West Indies in 1942. His description of the incident I quote in full, for it has certain other elements of comedy and farce which make it noteworthy.

As soon as Mobarak Ali was put on to bowl, the aforementioned umpire started no-balling him, and it mattered little what type of ball he bowled. He bowled his leg-breaks, and the umpire 'called', so finally he did an amazing thing. He started bowling underarm creepers, and for a time the match was reduced to a farce. In this riot of no balls Sealy actually lost his wicket, for expecting another no ball, he had a crack, was caught, and then found the umpire hadn't called. Ali continued to bowl, and eventually the no-balling ceased. Though he was probably quite right in a few of his decisions one cannot but say that 'our umpire' did rather overdo things.

—P. T. Thompson, *The Cricketer*

Mobarak Ali was 'called' thirty times!

It was not long after the reinstitution of cricket after the Second World War that the topic of doubtful bowling again rose. Cuan McCarthy played for South Africa against England in 1948–9 and 1951, and later went up to Cambridge, where he played for the university in the season of 1952.

He was a very tall man, and so loose of limb that some said he was double-jointed. His pace, in an era when only the Australians could boast a school of genuinely fast bowlers, was very considerable. His action, especially at moments of extra stress, was questionable, and there was a flexion of the arm during the last heave that could not be entirely explained by an extension of the joints. Writing at the time, I suggested that this was due to a premature turning of the trunk and shoulders when the bowler came to put a bit of added effort into his faster ball. Thus the bowler is showing his full chest to the batsman before his arm has started on the final swing. This is, to my mind, the basis of all illegitimate actions, and is another point into which I shall go more thoroughly when discussing the mechanics of bowling. McCarthy was, in fact, only no-balled once for throwing in this country, at Worcester, by Corrall, when playing for Cambridge University in 1952.

The fifties saw the emergence of Lock as an England bowler, and a highly controversial figure. When Lock came to the Oval in 1946 he was a slow left-hander of impeccable action, but with little power of spin. With a view to improving this he attended an indoor school, but found the overhead net too low to accommodate his lofty flight. He was thus compelled to flatten his trajectory and, in so doing, his action underwent some modification which much increased his spin. Armed with this he came to the top in 1952 when picked for England against India. But the pleasure of this advancement was abruptly menaced by W. F. Price, who, some days later, called him three times at the Oval for throwing, and from then on Lock was subject to considerable reservations.

In 1953–4 the M.C.C. toured the West Indies under the captaincy of Len Hutton. Lock was twice no-balled in the course of the tour. The first was in the opening Test match and in rather unfortunate circumstances. A fund had been organised by local enthusiasts to bring George Headley, the great batsman and hero of pre-war days, to play once again for his country. The arrangements were successfully completed and Headley duly appeared at Kingston, Jamaica. He made but 16 in the first innings of 417 and when he came in for a second time his side were far in the lead but at that moment had lost four wickets for 90 odd runs. Headley got off the mark with a single and then faced Lock's fast ball. Spectators say that he had only got about halfway through his generous and rather flourishing pick-up when the castle went down with a crash. The batsman's predominant reaction appeared to be one of bewilderment.

Jim Swanton wrote in his *West Indian Adventure* regarding the incident: 'The legitimacy of Lock's fast ball has been a matter of contention amongst cricketers since before he was no-balled at the Oval by Umpire Price, two years ago. It was a matter of more than abstract discussion in Lock's next over after Headley's departure, for he bowled another fast one to Gomez and umpire Perry Burke no-balled him from square leg.'

Later in the tour at Bridgetown, Barbados, Lock was again no-balled by both umpires, after which he used his faster ball at infrequent intervals.

In England Lock's victims were occasionally outspoken in their comments, but it was left to Douglas Insole to make one of the more devastating observations of the decade. When his castle was also wrecked by this thunderbolt with his bat still on the way up he passed a silent umpire on the way back. 'I know that was out,' he said. 'But was I bowled or run out?' Around this time the Australians had hard things to say of certain English institutions, one being our wickets and the other being Lock's action. Since he was accepted by English umpires, no official comment was made, but privately their opinion was, I suspect, unanimously to the effect that at any pace his action was wrong.

This, however, is a story with a happy ending. It is said that

Lock was greatly nonplussed on seeing a slow-motion film of himself in action, and determined to modify his action for the second time. It must have been a major undertaking for an established bowler to alter the habits of years, especially habits which had brought him such success. Lock is to be congratulated on the result of this courageous effort, for now he has an impeccable action and, although slower in pace, seems to have a most effective spin. His record with Western Australia in Sheffield Shield cricket would argue that he is a better performer on Australian pitches in his modified form than he was on May's trip with his debatable style.

Although Lock and McCarthy were the only two bowlers to be officially challenged in English cricket between the restart of the game after the end of the Second World War and 1959 there were a number of county bowlers who were spoken of as being far from perfect. There was sufficient uneasiness abroad to prompt some unofficial discussion at Lord's which led, in turn, to the inclusion of the question of throwing or jerking in the M.C.C. Cricket Sub-Committee's agenda for the meeting of February 1958. The result of the Sub-Committee's deliberations was that a message was passed to the first-class umpires' meeting in the following April urging their members to examine the actions of certain bowlers and, if necessary, to take firm steps under the provisions of Law 26. Despite this recommendation being officially endorsed by the full M.C.C. Committee, and supported by the Advisory Cricket Committee, it either failed to meet with any great response or the umpires were satisfied with all the bowlers they encountered in 1958, for not one was called during that season.

In the autumn the M.C.C. team under the captaincy of Peter May sailed for Australia, and soon the bitterest dispute between the cricketing communities of England and Australia since 'body-line' bowling had burst into the open.

Having seen the majority of the Australian suspects and having lived with the problem throughout the whole tour I had naturally given the matter a lot of thought. Apart from its technical complications it was a melancholy situation in that it inevitably gave rise toe nmity and suspicion between otherwise friendly or neutral parties and individuals. The English camp was unanimous in its conviction that there was an epidemic of illegal actions in Australia and that four Test-match bowlers were 'chuckers'. The most blatant was of least account. Jimmy Burke of New South Wales, a man as merry as his batting is staid, delivered his off-spinners (to my eyes) with the chopping bent-arm motion of a constable laying his truncheon on a very short offender's head. Slater of Western Australia was a border-line case and appeared in only one Test. Rorke was immensely fast and, with a skidding start, usually delivered from beyond the popping crease, with, at times, an obvious bend of the arm. But Meckiff was the central figure of the controversy.

When the M.C.C. arrived in Melbourne in November they had already viewed Slater at Perth, but had missed Hitchcox and Trethewey at Adelaide, where their unorthodox perform-ances occasionally evoked cries of 'strike one' and suchlike from the South Australian crowd. No one had actually seen Meckiff, but reports from South Africa had not been reassuring. The M.C.C. batted first, so that he was immediately on view, but, so far as the press was concerned, it was a distant one. The press box had been shifted to the new stand, so that the angle when Meckiff bowled from the pavilion end was from wide long-off, but about twice as deep and sixty feet up. At this distance and in this perspective Meckiff had a beautiful leisurely run-up which reminded me mildly of Ted McDonald. On arrival at the crease there was another similarity to that great bowler in the pause with the bowling arm poker straight at the horizontal. After that the swing was difficult to follow even with the aid of glasses, but the pace from this deceptively effortless performance was surprising. From what I had seen and from where I had seen it I could not form any conclusion beyond a suspicion that something between the perfection of the posture at the start of the swing and the delivery of the ball was not as it should be. This was deepened by the absence of any follow-through, so that the bowler finished standing still just in front of the crease. Others who saw him in the delivery action from different viewpoints, including the batting crease, had stronger opinions.

In December the first Test match was played at Brisbane. Arriving in the press box, I looked down and saw Meckiff turning his arm over gently to a batsman colleague. His action at that moment exactly resembled a coach throwing the ball to a young pupil in a net. Having watched this strange spectacle for some moments I turned to an Australian press colleague standing nearby and suggested that he was, of course, fooling and that this was not his normal action. My companion gave me a quizzical look. 'That is his action,' he said. It is fair to add that at such relaxed moments Meckiff's flex and bend was exaggerated and at normal speed these characteristics, although still distinguishable, were less pronounced. Even so, when the match started, and one saw him from directly behind, the result was disturbing.

The writer, especially on the visiting side, was in something of a dilemma. Meckiff was officially accepted by his own side and selectors and in the eyes of a great proportion of his fellow countrymen was a perfectly fair bowler. As England were soon in grave difficulties any adverse comment savoured of a 'squeal' and was vociferously denounced as such by certain sections of the Australian press and public. It was generally an unhappy atmosphere.

During the match I met Meckiff fleetingly in a group of players. A brief personal impression was of a typical young Aussie, which is to say a most personable and engaging young man of good manners and pleasant humour. This impression was borne out by all one heard of him from those who knew him more intimately. In all, this glimpse, and the supporting reputation, left me convinced of his complete honesty of purpose, if I could not accept that he was a fair and orthodox bowler according to my belief and experience.

All the home sympathisers did not accept him either. After

he had delivered a notably erratic over, to the accompaniment of some brilliant fielding by Harvey, a commentator gave tongue from the popular side. 'Put 'Arvey on', he shouted. 'At least he can throw straight.'

Local supporters were equally candid about the opening bowlers in the return match against South Australia at Adelaide. Trethewey and Hitchcox were greeted by jocular cries of 'strike one' by the Adelaidians and, on short acquaintance, named Trethrowy and Pitchcock by the visiting batsmen.

So to Melbourne, where the situation grew the more tense when Meckiff despatched England with six for 38 in the second innings. In the third Test at Sydney Meckiff was less effective, eventually retiring with tendon trouble in his leg; but the inclusion of Slater and a few overs of Burke kept the controversy to the fore.

With Meckiff injured Australia recalled Lindwall who had been quoted as jocularly saying that he was the last of the straight-arm Australian bowlers. With Davidson at the other end the Australian attack was opened by two of the most beautiful orthodox actions one could expect to see. The distraction this time was Rorke, whose elbow had a tendency to bend, and whose front foot came down as much as a yard in front of the popping crease. Despite a good first innings in which he took three for 23, it is doubtful if his presence was decisive when England went down, seething and frustrated once more, by ten wickets.

For the last match both Meckiff and Rorke were brought to Melbourne and took five wickets, again without being directly the determining factor in another heavy English defeat by nine wickets.

The result of the series—a 4–0 reverse—was the heaviest setback England had suffered since 1920–1. How far this margin was influenced by the unorthodoxy of the Australian attack was impossible to assess, but observers were quick to remark that Meckiff had headed the bowling averages, and the draw at Sydney was achieved by an English batting recovery, following his enforced withdrawal. What was beyond any doubt was

The premature turn of the chest and shoulders. Even one
as loosely jointed as Cuan McCarthy is going to have considerable
difficulty in maintaining full extension from the relative positions
of arm and trunk at this stage.

Ian Meckiff. In this photograph of Meckiff the reader may study the bend, the exaggerated arch of the back, the splayed foot, and, highly interesting, the position of the bowling hand. The last point is indicative of the unorthodox direction of the swing. See text, pages 56–57.

OPPOSITE **Meckiff in action against Cowdrey in the second Test match at Melbourne during the great controversy of 1958–9.** The elements of the action are identical with the above picture but have reached a fractionally later stage.

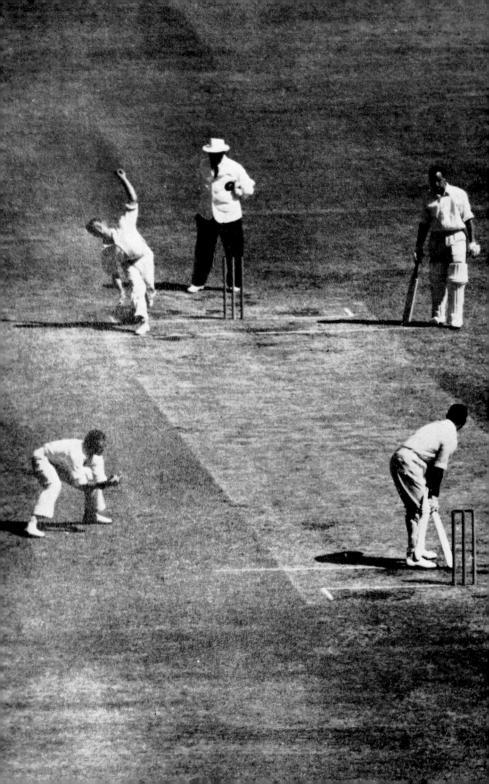

Ian Meckiff. A picture of historic interest taken in the first Test against South Africa at Brisbane, 12th December 1963, when he was finally no balled.

the unpleasant fact that an atmosphere had been generated in which the fruits of victory had been soured by doubt, and to the sting of defeat had been added the dilemma that any protest smacked of frustration.

But doubts there were on the Australian side and, be it to their credit, those subject to them were determined that they should be crystallised into action. Many suffered much embarrassment. When, in loyalty, and roused by English accusations they countered that, in Lock, we had our own sinner, they mostly shrank from the obvious answer to the question of why then was he not called by their umpires.

In this connection there was a possible by-product of these alarms and excursions which also caused one to ponder. During the previous tour of Australia in 1954–5 Mel McInnes had impressed all who saw him as one of the finest umpires in their experience. Firm, undemonstrative and immediate, he seemed to have a complete but unobtrusive command of the situation, which at all times ran smoothly. His second English series was a rather different story. Immediately he was the centre of controversy when, at Brisbane, Cowdrey was caught low on the ground by Kline and nobody, including the fielder himself, seemed to know the answer. Thereafter he appeared to be pursued by some demon of misfortune which, as his anxieties increased, seemed to delight in confronting him with difficulties. These culminated in a disaster at Adelaide when Colin McDonald had to seek the aid of a runner who, at one stage, stationed himself at point instead of square-leg. When an appeal was made against the substitute for a run-out McInnes found that he had his back turned upon the straining arrival, and so could offer no decision at all. Later, when Mackay was the subject of a particularly difficult catch to the wicket off bat and pad, it seemed that the umpire was incapable of reaching a verdict. The situation was resolved by that very generous cricketer walking out of his own volition. After these incidents McInnes was not reappointed for the last Test, a change which the English camp had been requesting ever since Brisbane. The matter did not end there, for McInnes was approached and wrote about the series in an Australian newspaper as soon as it was ended, thus setting a somewhat dubious precedent.

Having had a great regard for McInnes' professional ability I was sorry that things should have gone this way. Many comments and explanations were offered, but I myself felt that one most potent factor had been discounted. As senior umpire the already great weight of responsibility was increased to an impossible degree by the doubts or, more correctly, the outright accusations concerning the several Australian bowlers, and the counter-charges against Lock. McInnes was at least a fearless umpire; indeed, one of the charges against him was that he was too dictatorial. Had he been *convinced* of the illegality of any bowler's action he would certainly have intervened. He did in fact say that one ball from Lock at Brisbane he considered a throw and, had the batsman been out, he would have recalled him. 'This', wrote Jack Fingleton, 'is just not good enough', but it does give some idea of a confusion of mind arising at an early stage.

The point is that the most liberally minded observer must have seen that in, particularly, Meckiff's action there were certain peculiarities. In a mind as knowledgeable as that of McInnes it must have raised questions as seen from his privileged vantage point. One can only conclude that the malaise was so prevalent in Australia at that time that normally competent judgment was blurred. But in his case it could hardly be blurred to the point of complacency, and the constant strain of pondering a decision so fateful must have told on the sturdiest temperament. It is my case that it threw the finest exponent of his craft completely out of gear. If there is any substance in this supposition it makes the case for clear definition of law, to a point of unmistakable clarity, quite imperative.

The rumpus which arose out of the 1958–9 series was salutary in that it focused responsible authority in all cricketing countries upon the urgency of agreement on an elusive but potentially disastrous confusion. Not since body-line bowling had the two oldest and most influential cricketing powers been involved in such an inflammable situation.

A generation previously England had used the services of the greatest fast bowler in the world in what the majority of Australians, and a great number of Englishmen, considered was a violation of the spirit of the game of cricket. The controversies had certain points in common. They both devolved on a matter of opinion as against any precise point of legality under the existing code. They both aroused an unprecedented pitch of mutual recrimination. And, happily, they both, as far as was possible, were resolved by the good sense of both parties, and the tacit admission of the instigator that reflection had brought a doubt as to the fairness or otherwise of the instigation. Which is to say that body-line bowling was discouraged to the point of elimination by feeling in this country, and that Australians, once alive to the malaise of the chucker within their borders, were tireless in their efforts to deal with it.

In England M.C.C., as a result of deliberations inaugurated early in 1958, made a special appeal to umpires in March. It read as follows:

> The part of Law 26 which deals with throwing and jerking has been under discussion between M.C.C., the county committees and captains, and the first-class umpires since the winter of 1957–8. In the autumn of last year, it was unanimously agreed by the umpires that the action of certain bowlers in this country was, on occasion, suspect. The counties concerned have undertaken to warn these bowlers. The umpires have again been assured of the fullest support of M.C.C., the counties and the county captains in any action they may feel it necessary to take.

No bowler was called in England in 1958, but in 1959 the umpires suggested that a list should be compiled of suspect bowlers. M.C.C. gave their blessing and at the meeting of the Advisory County Cricket Committee the umpires were assured of full support and counties undertook to warn any of their bowlers who might figure on this list. The umpires let it be known that they did not consider a definition of a bowl or throw necessary, but asked for full official support in calling any bowler, whether listed or not.

In the meantime, however, the Australians had been extremely active and, as part of a determined campaign, had experimented with several possible definitions of a throw. As a result they submitted a suggestion that the words 'or jerked' should be removed from the phrasing of the law and a definition added to read:

> A ball shall be deemed to have been thrown if immediately prior to the delivery the elbow is bent with the wrist backward of the elbow, and the arm is then straightened as the ball is delivered. This definition of a throw does not debar the bowler from the use of the wrist in delivering the ball. Umpires are particularly directed to call and signal 'No ball' unless they are satisfied that the ball is bowled. The bowler shall not be given the benefit of the doubt.

It was not until November 1959 that M.C.C. agreed to experiment with the use of the Australian definition and, to aid these experiments in the season of 1960, re-phrased the Australian definition to read:

> A ball shall be deemed to have been thrown if, in the opinion of either umpire, there has been a sudden straightening of the bowling arm, whether partial or complete, immediately prior to the delivery of the ball. Immediately prior to the delivery of the ball will be taken to mean, at any time after the arm has risen above the level of the shoulder in the delivery swing. The bowler shall not be debarred from the use of the wrist in delivering the ball.

In 1960 the subject of unfair bowling was the main point upon the Imperial Cricket Conference agenda. The Australians considered it to be so important that Sir Donald Bradman undertook the trip himself, accompanied by Mr. W. J. Dowling. All the other countries were represented by senior members of their controlling bodies and the Conference got under way at

Lord's on 14th July 1960. Present were: R. Aird (Secretary, M.C.C.), H. H. Maharaja of Baroda (India), R. E. Foster Bowley (South Africa), A. H. H. Gilligan (New Zealand), A. Drayton (West Indies), Sir Donald Bradman (Australia), G. O. Allen (M.C.C.), H.E. Lt.-General Mohammed Yousuf (Pakistan), M. A. Chidambaram (India), J. St. F. Dare (West Indies), W. J. Dowling (Australia), H. S. Altham (President, M.C.C.), G. W. A. Chubb (South Africa), Sir Hubert Ashton (President Designate, M.C.C.) and Sir Arthur Sims (New Zealand).

The Conference announced on July 15th that it had unanimously agreed upon a definition of a throw to be used in all countries concerned. It was, as expected, an amalgam of the Australian and English drafts and in final form read:

> The ball shall be deemed to have been thrown if in the opinion of either umpire the bowling arm having been bent at the elbow (whether the wrist be backward of the elbow or not) is suddenly straightened immediately prior to the instant of delivery. The bowler shall, nevertheless, be at liberty to use the wrist freely in the delivery action.

As in the case of its components, this definition seemed to be lacking in the essential requirements of lucidity and brevity. The general instruction was complicated, and placed the weight of emphasis on the most difficult part of the action to detect with any certainty—the sudden straightening of the arm. The phrase 'immediately prior to delivery' was capable of a fairly generous interpretation in circumstances which called for firmness to the point of rigidity. It was a brave attempt to describe a throw, but inadequate for legal purposes, and so it was to prove in practice.

It had a further defect. It did not cover a very potent type of throw: the spinner who starts straight and shortens.

There was at this time a great deal of anxiety as to what might happen if Meckiff was picked for Australia and had to pass the English umpires thus exhorted and alerted. It was said

that his modified action was more in line with orthodox practice, but those who saw him in Australia felt the alteration
would have to be fairly basic if he was to pass unchallenged.
This, in fact, saved the day, for Meckiff in his new guise proved
much less effective and when the time came the question did
not arise (Meckiff, it may be remembered, attributed his loss
of form to injury, not change of style).

However, this was not to be known at the time and it was
thought expedient to forestall any recurrence of previous
dispute.

In November 1960 M.C.C. called a press conference at
which the President, Sir Hubert Ashton, took the chair. The
journalists present were then given details of an agreement
which had been negotiated with the Australian Board of
Control. It was worded as follows:

> M.C.C. and the English counties have agreed with the Austra-
> lian Board of Control for International Cricket to the following
> application of Law 26 during the Australian Tour to the United
> Kingdom in 1961:
>
> English umpires will be instructed not to call on the field for a
> suspect delivery (throwing) any Australian bowler on the 1961
> tour prior to June 7, 1961. Up to that date every umpire who
> officiates in an Australian match and who is not entirely satisfied
> of the absolute fairness of a delivery of any Australian bowler will,
> as soon as possible after the conclusion of each match, complete a
> confidential report on a form to be provided and send it to the
> President of M.C.C.—a duplicate copy to be sent through the
> Secretary of M.C.C. to the Manager of the Australian team. From
> June 7, 1961, the umpires will be instructed to implement Law 26
> on the field in the normal way, according to their own judgment;
> and the Australian bowlers will become 'liable' to be called for
> any infringement.
>
> At no stage of the tour will the bowler be, as it were, 'declared
> illegal' and he will be free to play as and when chosen at Australia's
> discretion.
>
> In view of the new definition of a throw and the agreement
> referred to above, the M.C.C. and the English counties will con-

sider whether or not to adopt the same procedure in all first-class matches prior to June 7, 1961.

The Umpire's Report is set out thus:

CONFIDENTIAL   FORM 'A'

UMPIRE'S REPORT

To the President
M.C.C.

I beg to report that I officiated at the match Australia *v.*
.....................played on..........(date) at........
....

In my opinion the Australian bowler...............(name) infringed Law 26 (Throwing) in this match to the following degree:

☐ Basically—that is every ball.
☐ Frequently.
☐ Occasionally.
☐ Very rarely.

(Please mark category thus [**X**] and make any comments you may wish and especially any which you think may help the bowler concerned.)

Yours faithfully,

In effect this was a truce and was received with some surprise and a certain amount of doubt. The general feeling was that even if there were some unsatisfactory aspects of the efforts made to deal with throwing the concerted determination of those concerned and the courage and firmness of the leading umpires had produced material results. To relax these efforts, at the highest level, even for a limited time, seemed a dubious step.

In assessing the desirability and value of this truce, however, it is proper to do so against the circumstances prevailing at that particular time, including the great publicity being given to the controversy. Australia had taken a leading part in the campaign to rid the game of illegal bowling, but at this stage there were still four possible selections for the tour of England whose actions, whilst they had not actually been condemned, could have been highly suspect in some quarters. Had they been included and had they been called by English umpires there could well have been a repetition of the previous row, and the whole tour utterly ruined at the very outset. It was thought that if these bowlers came to England a truce would give all parties a breathing space during which any Australian bowler whose action failed to satisfy the English umpires would have a reasonable opportunity of adjusting his action to satisfy their interpretation. If this proved impossible at least the offender would not have been dismissed without a reasonable and extended trial. Those who supported the truce strongly emphasised that an international tour should not be jeopardised just because an English umpire might interpret the law somewhat differently from an Australian umpire. The English bowlers were in somewhat different case, as they would merely be continuing to operate before the same umpires who had previously observed them.

Whether the benefits of the truce would have outweighed the objections had a doubtful case arisen must remain a matter of surmise for not one of the quartette was selected, and the Australian bowlers were orthodox and blameless to a man.

Meantime on the field of play there had been considerable repercussions, and some significant incidents. Almost unnoticed against the turbulent events elsewhere, a promising young South African bowler named Griffin had been no-balled on two occasions, playing for Natal in South African domestic cricket. The first of these was on his home ground of Durban bowling against the Transvaal, and the second in an away match against Border and Eastern Province at East London.

There was a stronger crusading spirit amongst English um-

pires at the start of the home season of 1959. For some time
Pearson, one of Worcestershire's opening fast bowlers, had been
eyed with suspicion from a number of quarters but had, only
once been the subject of official censure. In the first match of
the Indians' tour, at Worcester in April, Buller called him in
the first innings, but, presumably, Pearson modified his methods, for he continued to bowl and wound up with five wickets.
In mid-May he was again called on the same ground whilst
playing against Essex.

Another Worcestershire opening bowler, Aldridge, ran into
trouble in July at Kidderminster in the match against Leicestershire. Aldridge, who had played for Kidderminster before join-
ing the county, had a crowded hour on this familiar stage. He
hit three towering sixes in making 19 runs, started with three
wickets for two runs, and was no-balled by Buller for throwing.
Earlier in the month Lock had again been called, by umpire
Gibb, at Cardiff. This concluded the list of prosecutions in
England and, despite the great vigilance, only one case arose in
Australia in the following months. This was J. McLaughlin,
playing for Queensland against New South Wales at Sydney.

In England in 1960 there were forty-seven officially recognised throws, the greatest number ever recorded in one season
of first-class cricket in any country. The major proportion of
this total came from the young South African fast bowler
Griffin. Elsewhere I have written about this rather sad case in
more detail, but his brief and stormy career is probably still
fairly fresh in the minds of cricket followers. I remember going
to Ilford to see the South Africans play Essex early in their tour.
Griffin opened the bowling, giving to the press tent a sideways-
on front view of his action. I was much perturbed by what I saw
and another look from the screen towards which he was bowling
emphasised that there was something amiss. Neither umpire
took any action but both watched him with the keenest interest.
Perhaps both were uneasily conscious of the fact that no visitor
to this country with a touring side had ever been called for
illegal bowling.

E

It was not until the 21st of May, when the South Africans came to Lord's to play the M.C.C., the most important match of the tour outside the actual series, that this happy record was broken. The umpires concerned were Frank Lee and John Langridge, both senior and responsible officials, with wide practical experience as players and umpires. In M.C.C.'s first innings Lee called Griffin once and Langridge did so twice. Once when Langridge called him for throwing, Lee, from the bowler's end, called him for dragging over the line, thereby also creating a precedent, for, so far as I know, never before had a bowler been condemned simultaneously on both counts. Going to Nottingham later in May, Griffin was no-balled again, this time on eight counts by Bartley and Copson.

An intensive three-day course with Alf Gover seemed to have greatly improved Griffin's action from the legal standpoint but at the inevitable cost of some of his life and devil. After a leanish period which included the first Test it seemed that Griffin's troubles, as far as umpires were concerned, might be over, but at Southampton on June 20 and 21 both umpires, J. H. Parks and Harry Elliott, intervened, once each in the first innings and four times in the second. Despite this set-back Griffin was included in the side for the second Test match at Lord's. England's only innings brought him the most extraordinary variations of fortune. He took four wickets, was the first of his countrymen ever to do a hat-trick in a Test match, and was no-balled eleven times by Frank Lee.

What would have happened had this particular matter ended there is difficult to say, but, owing to the premature ending of the main event, an exhibition match was arranged as promised in such a contingency. This time Griffin bowled for the first time with Buller standing at square-leg and it was immediately clear this was the most crucial test the bowler had yet faced. When Buller had rejected four of the first five balls bowled it was apparent that this was the end of Griffin's career, just as Phillips had passed sentence on Mold those many years before. So it proved to be, for when the over had been completed underhand there could be no question of Griffin's action being accepted henceforth. It was, as I have said, a sad moment.

There were four previous offenders amongst the other seven cases in this season. Lock was again no-balled early on at Cambridge. Aldridge was called at Pontypridd and his opposite number, Pearson, at Dudley against Northamptonshire. Rhodes encountered Gibb in the match against the South Africans at Derby and was called six times.

A young left-hander, Bryant, had his career cut short whilst playing for Somerset against Gloucestershire at Bath, where Yarnold objected to four balls in one over. White of Hants was no-balled by Gibb at Hove, twice in the first innings and once in the second. The last case was by comparison not an important one, R. T. Simpson, of Notts, playfully throwing the last ball of the match against Derbyshire at Trent Bridge.

At the moment of writing Griffith is, and has been for the past few years, the most controversial figure in international cricket. As a personality and as a bowler he is something of an enigma.

His cricketing career has from its beginnings been eventful. He started as a wicket-keeper and batsman. From this he became a slow off-spin bowler. On graduating to the Empire Club, which boasted Weekes and Hunte amongst its members, he became a fast bowler for the very good reason that the team did not have one handy at that particular moment. This turned out to be a very happy shortage in its effects for all concerned. It did not take as able a judge as Weekes long to see that the volunteer was more than adequate for the post.

The next advancement was to the ranks of Barbados, which can share with New South Wales the claim to being the most powerful centre, as a continuous and going concern, in the cricket world. Thence Griffith arrived in the topmost grade when he was picked for the West Indies in the final Test match against Peter May's team in 1960 at Port of Spain, Trinidad.

No great sensation was connected with this first appearance. He shared the new ball with Hall, being preferred to Watson, who had been the chief support in the previous matches. His only success came right at the start of the match when he had Pullar caught in the slips off a bouncer to take the first wicket of the day. At the time I wrote: 'The new fast bowler had a nice, supple wheeling action, rather like his namesake or Francis of a generation ago. His pace was not devastating but he got a lot of bounce when he dropped short, and appeared to bring the ball into the batsman. When the score was 19 he had his first success when he bowled a bouncer at Pullar, who seemed to be late in picking up the flight of the ball, and was caught in the slips off his gloves.' All of which makes quite interesting reading in light of later events.

In 1961–2 the Indians toured the West Indies and lost every Test match in the series of five. They suffered, as over many years, from one major deficiency, which was a particular disadvantage in the Caribbean. For a number of reasons pertaining to diet, physique and possibly climate, India has not produced a real fast bowler since the large and sturdy Mohammed Nissar. They have produced many fine bowlers of other types, but lack of genuine pace is a double-edged disadvantage. In the first place batsmen do not get the practice and experience to enable them to cope with opposing pacemen, and secondly there is no means of retaliation if they suffer from any undue exuberance from that quarter.

In 1962 Hall and Griffith were the fastest pair of bowlers in the game, and Watson and several others were available in reserve. In the Barbados match at Bridgetown Griffith hit Contractor on the head and fractured his skull. Whilst the batsman lay in dire peril of his life in hospital Griffith was called for throwing. It was, to say the least of it, a melancholy interlude, but happily Contractor survived. His colleagues could not but be filled with doubt.

The West Indian side started its tour of England at Arundel Castle in April 1963, and Griffith was seen in England for the first time. Richie Benaud played for the Duke of Norfolk's side, and batted for about forty minutes before falling to Griffith's yorker. His comment next day was that it seemed to come more quickly than one might expect, adding that this might be attributed to the bowler's outsize physique. Whatever the reason the yorker was soon to become famous.

Early in the season the *Sunday Times* proposed to do a strip cartoon of Griffith, showing his early career, and asked if I would see him and get the necessary details. With the help of Berkeley Gaskin, the manager, a meeting was arranged at Old Trafford. At this stage of his career I found Griffith a quiet, rather shy young man who talked with affection about his days in West Indian club cricket. Apart from the ill-starred Barbados match against the Indians, there had been no general mutterings about his action, and he was clearly without resentment or suspicion.

Soon after this came the first objections, and these grew more outspoken as the tour progressed. Griffith had an immensely successful trip in Test and county matches and finished the season with 119 wickets at 12·83 apiece, far ahead of his fellows. He was not called on any occasion for throwing, but the editor of *Wisden*, ever alert, had some pointed things to say in his annual notes. 'At times the England batsmen found Griffith, with no sight-screen behind him, nasty with his ability to mix the yorker and the bouncer. Some people questioned whether his arm was bent when he put down his quicker and shorter ball. Instead of a full arm swing from which the batsman judges the pace of the ball and its length, there was occasionally a reduced arm swing and that meant that the ball did not have the length expected.' *Wisden* also had some adverse comments to make on his use of the bouncer, which reached a pitch in the final Test match which caused Buller to intervene twice on the first day.

Returning to the West Indies Griffith had another good season and for the moment the arguments died down. But in the spring of 1965 the Australians toured the Caribbean and soon feeling mounted to a hitherto unequalled intensity. The Australians were convinced that Griffith threw both his bouncer and quick yorker. No official voice was raised, but the press, led by Richie Benaud, stated their views without reservation. Benaud took a great number of photographs to support his case and, to an unbiased eye, several were such that they could leave no doubt that the action could not be passed as a bowl—if one applied the test of the extended arm above the horizontal. The illustration reproduced opposite page 64 was taken at Kingston in the first Test match and clearly depicts every characteristic associated with the chucker, enumerated later in this book. O'Neill wrote a series of press articles at the end of the tour in such outspoken terms that they evoked an official complaint from the President of the West Indies Cricket Board. It was a thoroughly unhappy situation, and not a very good prelude to the West Indian tour of England in the following year.

On meeting Griffith again, it struck me that events had made some impact upon his personality, and that the shy, engaging youth of three years before had grown into a reserved and somewhat prickly man. Those who played against him remarked that he was touchy and sombre in contrast to the ebullient good nature of Hall, who, when Milburn hit his bouncer with the new ball for six, gave the batsman a personal round of applause. He was clearly and understandably very resentful of the point-blank accusations made against him by leading players in every country against which he had played. There was naturally a great impatience to see him at work again so that every interested party in this country could reassess his case.

Griffith's first appearance in a first-class match was at Oxford against the University on May 7th. Oxford batted first and I was able to get a very good view from the press box, which was actually situated in the pavilion, almost directly in line with the wickets. Griffith bowled from the opposite end, so that one had an advantageous perspective from which to see any unorthodoxy in his action. For the *Sunday Times* I wrote: 'In his first appearance as a bowler during the present West

Indies tour Griffith made a splendid and impressive spectacle at Oxford, surging up and wheeling away with a fine, massive rhythm.

'On this form, it was a model fast bowler's action.'

Griffith's next appearance was at Lord's against the M.C.C. where he had a lean match with one wicket for 73 runs, but satisfied both Copson and Yarnold who stood umpire. Going to Old Trafford, Griffith met with mixed fortunes, and was the centre of a strange incident. He took the only four Lancashire wickets to fall at the modest cost of 55 runs out of a total of 296. In the process he was called no less than eight times for overstepping the crease and once, by umpire Fagg, for throwing. The strange incident was that, although there were a number of journalists present whose main interest was to observe Griffith, the call for throwing went by unnoticed. It was only the next day that the Lancashire players drew attention to the facts, and there was much speculation, and some chagrin, amongst the writers who had missed this very important point. The first explanation was that Fagg's call had gone unnoticed because it coincided with one of the eight calls for overstepping. Had this been so it would have been a very remarkable incident, and one of the rare cases of a bowler being called for two offences arising from the same ball. Further investigation disproved this theory, and how the offence went unnoticed, except on the field, remained something of a mystery.

It was not until the fourth Test match at Leeds that there was any further official comment on Griffith's action. He had bowled steadily and well through the trip but had never been the devastating force of 1963. This was reflected in a fair-to-middling record of eleven wickets at just under 25 apiece in three Test matches. It was noticeable that whereas he had established himself as the spearhead of the attack on the previous trip, Sobers now often preferred to share the new ball with Hall himself.

At Leeds, however, Griffith was restored to the opening partnership but was far outshone by Hall who found his best form and produced a tremendous sustained pace. It is possible that Griffith may have been affected by this disparity, for when the score was 18 for two he released a bouncer at Graveney which for venom and action made everyone gasp. It was immediately apparent that it had caused considerable disturbance on the field. The umpires conferred and it was afterwards related that Elliott said to Buller that in his opinion the delivery had been illegal, and it was agreed that he should speak to Griffith. The words he used he afterwards stated were: 'You can bowl, Charlie. Any more like that and I will have to call you. That delivery to Graveney was illegal.'

There can be no doubt that, however diplomatic he may have been, Elliott was wrong in law. Griffith should have been called without ado. Perhaps this is to be pedantic, for the net cost was one run to England. But in dealing with a matter so delicate it is advisable to stick to the book.

The result was in fact satisfactory, and *Wisden* comments that 'Following the incident much of Griffith's pace disappeared and he took only one more wicket in the match when D'Oliveira skied a loose ball to cover.'

At the Oval Griffith took one for 78 in England's total of 527, so finished the tour with a record of 14 wickets in Test matches at 31·28 a time and 49 wickets in all first-class matches at 20·36.

Where at this moment does Griffith stand regarding the fairness or otherwise of his action? My own judgment, which, I trust, is dispassionate and technical, is that at cruising pace his action is perfectly orthodox. His extra-fast ball is beyond doubt a throw. Of the cause of this I am also fairly certain. It is again the premature turn of the trunk and shoulders prompted by the sudden increase of effort. From this position the inevitable development is the javelin or shot putter's action. Should anyone wish to form his own judgment on these opinions he may study the pictures opposite page 64.

––––––––––

The case of Harold Rhodes arose some time before that of

G. A. R. Lock—Surrey II v Wiltshire, 1953. A revealing picture showing the fingers at the end of release while the bent elbow is in the process of straightening.

H. J. Rhodes—Derbyshire v Northamptonshire, 1965. This picture illustrates the difficulty of assessing the legality of an action from the side view. The double-jointed arm at full extension may well have a backward bend but comply with the proposed 'horizontal law'. In order to throw, the arm must, at the appropriate moment, be bent upwards towards the shoulder, and thus would be readily discernible from a front view. On the evidence of this particular picture, it is only possible to return an open verdict.

G. A. R. Lock. The modified action which Lock achieved after being disturbed by the study of film-shots of his original action. Here the arm is extended and the position of chest and shoulder perfectly co-ordinated.

G. M. Griffin. The bent arm above the horizontal. Under the suggested law, this would be a no-ball whether or not there was any subsequent straightening.

Griffith but has run concurrently with it for the past few years and has proved, if anything, more controversial. Rhodes, the son of the old Derbyshire leg-spinner, started with his county as far back as 1953. Originally a spin bowler, he altered his style and so became a fast right-handed seam bowler, a type in which Derby have been particularly rich over the years. When Rhodes was picked to play for England in 1959 against India it looked as if he might be the best of the line since Copson and George Pope.

Unfortunately there had always been some doubt concerning his action and the matter was complicated by a considerable backward extension of the elbow joint. It was urged in favour of Rhodes that this peculiarity automatically gave his action a suspect look, but that his delivery was perfectly fair. There was no general agreement on this point and whilst bowling against the South Africans at Derby in 1960 Rhodes was called by P. A. Gibb six times. This brought to official notice a controversy which to this day remains largely unsolved. Although a most successful bowler in county cricket Rhodes was suspect in some quarters, again called by Gibb in 1961, and not selected again for England or any official tour abroad. The suspicions were further crystallised when at Chesterfield in June 1965 Buller twice called Rhodes for throwing in the South Africans' second innings. As so often, this intervention caused keen resentment among certain sections of the public and there followed the strange spectacle of an English umpire being protected by the police from possible assault by a sober English cricket crowd.

In 1966 the M.C.C. Sub-Committee, appointed for the purpose of adjudicating in doubted cases, made a close study of Rhodes' action, including a film in which the elusive arm was painted black on one side and white on the other, to clarify its exact path and rotation. The Committee were generally satisfied that it was a fair delivery, and a statement was issued which read: 'The Committee unanimously considered the basic action to be fair, but were divided on the evidence before them as to whether or not his action was occasionally suspect. They intend, therefore, to have further films taken and hold another meeting.'

This took place in June, when the Committee accepted his basic action as fair, although they were divided as to whether or not an occasional delivery contravened the law. Thus poor Rhodes was left like Mahomet, suspended between Heaven and Hell.

Not long ago I had a most interesting talk with Rhodes and was given an opportunity of inspecting the extension of the joint at close quarters. This, although very pronounced, was not as great as I had anticipated.

Rhodes was completely and sincerely convinced of the fairness of his action, and wholly convinced that suspicion was erroneously based on this unusual effect created by the backward bend of his arm when it came over at full extension.

Having listened with great interest to the bowler's own views, I then studied him through field glasses from various angles. This, combined with the evidence of several film shots, has strengthened my own opinion of this unusual and very difficult case. It is that the extension of the joint is largely irrelevant. I believe that Rhodes is in fact subject to exactly the same forces which govern the delivery of any bowler of normal elbow extension. That is to say when he is bowling within himself his action is perfectly orthodox. But when he puts in an extra effort he does occasionally rotate his shoulders prematurely and there is a bend and flex in the arm. The bend is exactly as the normal arm when about to throw, which must be upwards and inwards. I am equally convinced that Rhodes is completely unaware of this process, which is the unconscious result of the extra thrust of the right shoulder. I also believe it could be eradicated, or could have been, by certain minor alterations in the arm swing and gradual elimination of the premature turn of the trunk. In fairness, it should be added, when I have fancied that I have seen the bend, in Rhodes' case it has not been exaggerated. This, however, has probably contributed to the indecision which has made his case so vexing to all concerned, especially Rhodes himself.

There is a further point to be considered regarding Rhodes.
A number of people who have studied his action in life and on
film point out that his arm, possibly with the momentum of a
lusty swing, straightens from the backward extension to the
straight as it comes over. This they say is not a throw but would
be a no-ball under the 'horizontal law'. Which is true—although it is unlikely that this comparatively small movement
would either be detectable or have any effect in practice. But
the answer is perfectly simple and it is to keep the arm fully
extended until the ball is released. This provision can be
observed by any bowler whatever the degree of movement he
may have in his elbow. I have returned to this point on page
75 when discussing the report of the M.C.C. Sub-Committee.

The Mechanics

John Arlott writing in the *Law Journal* has said that to produce a definition of a throw was more a job for a lawyer and an anatomist than a cricketer. This is very true, provided the lawyer could put his findings into simple layman's language, for the problem is essentially one of mechanics and anatomy.

Some people question the necessity for any definition at all, on the ground that anyone can recognise a throw as against a bowl. But this trusting belief has been shown to be fallacious in practice. Rather is it true to say that anyone can recognise what he considers to be throwing as opposed to bowling. When Meckiff's action was questioned by English pressmen there was a great outcry in the Australian press and public. Standards had grown lax and thousands of honest observers, accustomed to this drift, *genuinely* believed that Meckiff was an orthodox practitioner assailed by a disgruntled partisan body frustrated in defeat. When umpire Buller in 1965 no-balled Rhodes at Chesterfield he had to be given police protection from a normally staid English cricket crowd. Any criticism of Griffith is liable to meet with considerable indignation in West Indian circles. There are many other examples where this issue is confused and criticism is attributed to bias on grounds of race, team or nation by people who, not seeing anything amiss in the offender's action, can find no other explanation. Pity the poor umpire who is merely saying that he is not fully satisfied. Without any *factual* ruling to fall back upon he is rather like a judge told that there is no law upon the case at issue, but to use his discretion and, if his decision starts a riot, to keep smiling.

If the definition upon which his decision, and its justification, will rest is to be of material help it must obviously fulfil certain basic requirements. In the first place it must be applied to some instantly recognisable feature which distinguishes between bowl and throw. It must be simple and lucid, so as to be applicable on the spot in the very short time available. It must cover all contingencies. It is desirable that the reason for disqualification should be apparent to all present.

In order to formulate a definition to meet all these requirements it is necessary to consider the essential differences in the action accepted as bowling, and that which is clearly throwing or, as in baseball, pitching.

Round-arm or over-arm bowling is a combination of momentum, gathered from a running start, and the sling of the arm, augmented by the turn of the shoulders and the bend of the back. The question of momentum is of the greatest importance, for, although it is possible to bowl the ball some distance from a standstill, it is quite impossible to achieve any pace. Almost every fast bowler of unquestionable delivery has run over a dozen yards, as it is desirable to gain momentum progressively if the bowler is to be sufficiently balanced and co-ordinated to utilise it when he reaches the crease. A notable exception was Walter Brearley, of Lancashire, who ran only about seven yards, but was endowed with such strength of thigh that he could leap over a billiard table from a standing start. Even so, he would hardly qualify for the highest class in terms of pure pace. Momentum, if in a lesser degree, is essential to the slower bowler, for to spin and propel the ball twenty-two yards takes considerable effort.

The bowling action is in essence a very simple movement, but, to achieve its perfection, calls for a degree of rhythm and co-ordination of the most exact and unusual order. To bowl at the pace of Larwood or Hall is an enormous physical feat, and to spin with the accuracy of Barnes or O'Reilly a matter of quite exceptional dexterity.

Throwing is a rather more complicated movement, but, paradoxically, much more easily acquired up to a reasonable degree of proficiency. There are many more good throwers than good bowlers, and, whilst many good bowlers have been able to throw, there are a great number of first-class throwers who make little success at bowling. The action of a throw calls for a modicum of momentum, but is dependent to a much greater extent on a sudden burst of muscular exertion, the bend of the back combining with the flexion of shoulder, elbow and wrist to give a catapulting effect. Thus it is possible to produce great power from a stationary position, as the baseball pitcher amply demonstrates. But, in passing, it is worth noting that the pitcher is made to throw from a static stance, as a safeguard. Were he allowed complete freedom in the matter it is certain he would not avail himself of a bowler's run-up, as this would tend to upset his co-ordination. When one wants to throw a maximum pace or span the instinctive procedure is not to run an un-limited distance but to advance a few steps, broadly in the rhythm of one-two-three-four—bang. This undoubtedly sup-plies a certain amount of momentum, but its chief purpose is the extension of the trunk and limbs to the point of the utmost purchase and, in so doing, provides a great advantage over the pitcher's stationary wind-up. This is a convenient stage to underline this point which has a strong bearing on the mechanics of throwing, as applied to the illegitimate bowler, and to which I shall later revert.

Perhaps a reasonable comparison between the different techniques of bowling and throwing would be to liken the first to the swinging, sweeping motion of the flail as against the flicking of the whip, the human trunk providing the shaft in both cases, and the arm the lash.

As in bowling actions, there are a thousand variations in the motions of different throwers, but there are also several basic types. There is the flat, shoulder-high flip seen to perfection in the case of Neil Harvey. There is the wind-up and full over-arm hurl designed for great distance as practised by O'Neill. But these methods applied to 'bowling' would be so obvious that no argument would arise. The commonest infringement where bowling and throwing become intermixed is a species of heave between a javelin thrower and a shot putter. The reason for this can be seen by the study of the 'chucker' in action, and certain symptoms are always apparent in the actual performance or from judiciously timed photographs.

The vital moment where the thrower diverges from the orthodox bowler is at a comparatively late stage on the last stride as the propeller sets himself for the final heave. Pictures of the great orthodox actions, of Larwood, Lindwall, Bedser or Tate, are almost identical in major features at this point. The trunk is sideways, the left shoulder, pulled up and across by a fully extended left arm which makes an almost straight line through the shoulders to the fully extended right arm. The completion of the action consists in this perfectly co-ordinated arrival of the front foot, the turn of the waist and shoulders to carry the straight swinging arm through to the point of release and follow-through.

Now should the performer, by chance or design, alter the timing of the sequence immediately preceding the final position the result is rather different. If at the point described the bowler has started the turning of the trunk too soon his chest, as against his left shoulder, will be presented to the batsman by the time his right arm has reached the ordinary position for the final heave, normally at an angle of 45 degrees or more below the horizontal. Unless the subject is double-jointed he will find it impossible to get his *extended* arm from that position higher than round-arm. If he wants to achieve the perpendicular he must bend and straighten and if athletic will derive great propulsive power from this flexion. The reader can demonstrate this point for himself with greater clarity than I can convey by word. If you stand sideways, feet widely extended, and stretch your arms out like the sails of a windmill, starting with the right arm at about forty-five degrees below the horizontal, you can swing over the top with ease. If, keeping the arms in the original position, you turn the trunk and shoulders then try, you will, quite painfully, realise the force of the argument.

This provides a reasonable explanation of why the fair bowler may unwittingly throw on occasions. The increased effort to bowl a faster ball, or dig in a bouncer, can lead to this premature turn of the trunk and thrust of the right shoulder and the consequent lock of the bowling arm so that the bowler is bound to bend and flex. A case in point was Loader of Surrey, whose fast bouncer was suspect, and occasionally clearly a throw. Loader was completely honest in the matter and was quoted as saying that, although he had no evil intentions, he was sometimes aware that he had thrown the ball, *after* it had gone.

The premature turn which leads to this particular type of infringement produces certain symptoms which are indicative of the thrower although not necessarily conclusive in themselves. The action is naturally full-fronted and the line of the feet is inclined to splay in the direction of the slips, as against the case of the orthodox action which brings the footmarks of the operative stride in a line pointing to fine leg or at least straight-ahead. Whereas the toe of the leading foot in normal circumstances points straight down the line of the wicket, the front foot in the case of the thrower is frequently cocked in the direction of cover-point. The reader who tries the suggested experiment will find that the front foot inclines to turn and cock in sympathy with the premature turn of the shoulders. This premature turn of the trunk and consequent tensioning of the shoulder and muscles of the right arm also leads to an exaggerated arching of the back. In the case of the seamer, or fast bowler, the position of the hand is also indicative, for the fingers must be behind the ball in relation to the direction of the thrust. Thus, in a full circular sweep, the ball is seen by the batsman in a consistent path with the fingers and palm behind it. In the case of the chuck the hand and ball do not trace a consistent arc but, with the bend of the arm, loop to a position somewhere behind the bowler's head and flip out again. At this point the thrower's hand is turned and cocked so that the palm of the hand is facing towards mid-on. This is a position which no orthodox seam bowler's hand would normally achieve and, although a spinner's hand can certainly do so, it is the result of an entirely different grip and process, and does not bear upon the argument. The illustrations will help explain these points, which may sound somewhat complex in my attempts to explain them. Each one is clearly to be seen in the photographs of Mekiff at Melbourne between pages 32 and 33.

There is another significant characteristic. The bowler's momentum must be finally dissipated in a follow-through which usually carries him well past the wicket in the direction of cover-point. To the thrower this excess of momentum is unnecessary and possibly a disadvantage. His inclination is to pause at the delivery stage, and the forward urge is largely dispersed at the moment when the ball is released. The result is a noticeable absence of the normal bowler's run-out, and the thrower can end up quite comfortably a yard or so in front of the crease. In this context the length of run is not particularly relevant, but, where to the bowler acceleration at the point of delivery is important, the thrower tends to decelerate. Because of this the thrower can operate off a short run which, to the fast bowler, would be quite inadequate. In his book Meckiff cites the fact that he ran as far as most of the great fast bowlers. But in his case the run, although rhythmical, was leisurely and there was a distinct pause, or at least an absence of hustle, just before and on the delivery stride. There was little, if any, follow-through in the normal sense of the term.

It is sometimes argued that the bowler who starts his swing from the classic sideways position cannot throw. This is not wholly true, for many photographs of baseball pitchers reveal a beautiful preliminary position for a bowl, always allowing for the exaggerated position of the front leg in compensation for lack of momentum. The pitcher is, of course, winding up from

F

a standing start for the full-blooded throw as practised by out-fields which, as I have endeavoured to show, differs from the shot-putter-cum-javelin throw which constitutes the cricket 'chucker'. As I have said, anyone who employed the pitcher's action from the bowling crease would be so obviously divorced from a genuine bowler that no problem would arise. From this it would, therefore, be true to say that it is very much more difficult to confuse bowl and throw in the case of one who preserves the classic sideways delivery. Without complicating the matter to the point of obscurity it may be described as largely one of timing, for the most orthodox bowler must show his full front to the batsman at some point. But this point is reached roughly when the arm is approaching the vertical. If it is reached *before* the horizontal the arm cannot come over the top unless bent at the elbow. The one unarguable point is that in order to throw it is necessary to bend the arm. This is the focus of all controversy, for some say that it is possible to bend the arm and still be a fair bowler.

When the authorities concerned, particularly in England and Australia, decided that, in view of the situation, a definition to clarify the law was desirable they were faced with two obvious choices. They could define a throw or they could define a bowl. After due consideration it was decided to take the former course, and much thought was given to the extremely difficult problem of describing what constituted a throw within the context of bowling.

The Horizontal Law

Writing for the *Sunday Times* in the midst of the controversy in Australia I appealed for some definition of a bowl or throw to qualify the law in the clearest possible terms. I suggested that, as a basis for discussion, such definition of a bowl should be that when the hand reached the level of the shoulder the arm should be fully extended until the ball was released. I still believe that, translated into precise terms, this is the simplest and most effective way of qualifying the law.

The more legalistic wording would read: 'When the arm reaches the horizontal on the final swing it will be fully extended until the ball is released.' In order to ensure that the bowler can use his wrist without restriction, the words 'from shoulder to wrist' might be inserted after 'fully extended', but the shorter and simpler the definition the better.

The case for this definition comprises several points. It satisfies the first requirement of simplicity. The umpire has to concern himself with but one simple fact—was the arm bent above the horizontal? It may be argued that this from certain angles is not easy to decide. But seen from the batsman's vantage point it is impossible to disguise any flexion sufficient to enable anyone to throw. The umpire, if suspicious, would be allowed to move his position towards fine-leg slip, and any resultant loss would rightly devolve upon the bowler or bowling. In any case it is to be borne in mind that if no bend is detectable it is quite certain that no sudden straightening will be seen.

The umpire having seen a bend of the arm above the horizontal would immediately call 'no-ball' whatever the bowler did thereafter. If called upon for any explanation he would only have to state that the arm was not fully extended, and there could be no further argument, for this would in itself have contravened the law. Partisan spectators like those who, in the past, have demonstrated against umpires brave enough to commit themselves under the present legislation would be in no better case to dispute a decision made in this case than in one of lbw. To those in a position to see, the reason for the decision would be apparent. But the most important matter is that the umpire would be making an impersonal judgment of fact, without reflection on character or intent, and, as I have said, have concrete reason to offer for his decision, as against a general expression of opinion.

It must be beyond dispute that observance of this law would completely rule out any type of throwing. It is, of course, wise to remember once again that only practical trial would determine how well it would work when applied in actual use.

From my own observation of a number of suspect actions, several subsequently officially convicted, I would think its application would be perfectly simple and reliable in the hands of an experienced judge. It is directed at the essential and initial movement in throwing, as opposed to bowling, and at the same time the most discernible. There is a further point which may have a slightly Irish logicality. It is this. If anyone is convinced he has seen a blatant throw he may be quite sure, without making a detailed study, that the arm has been bent above the horizontal. What is also beyond doubt is that a generation brought up strictly under the requirements of the 'horizontal law' will produce no 'chuckers' at all.

Although not privy to the deliberations of the Imperial (now International) Cricket Conference, and the workings of the various sub-committees engaged on this subject, one can be certain that the possibility of defining a bowl, as against a throw, was most thoroughly examined. In their report the I.C.C. stated that the objection to the fully extended arm was that it would handicap the genuine bent-arm bowler. This to me has always been, and remains, an untenable objection for a number of specific reasons.

The existence of a legitimate bent-arm bowler is, in the first place, debatable. The only visibly bent arms I have seen have in every case belonged to 'chuckers'. In the case of several spinners there may be a slight relaxation or a tendency to shorten at the end of the swing in order to impart more snap. The Australians made some investigation into this, but were satisfied that the actions of Benaud, Laker and other spinners of leg- and off-breaks were impeccable. Any impression of flexion came from the exaggerated lock and turn of the wrist. All the truly great bowlers of any type have been straight arm, whatever their type or pace. Barnes, Lindwall, Rhodes, O'Reilly, Bedser, all had the full sweep of an extended arm which, for the requirements of spin, and swerve and, notably, for consistent accuracy, is the most effective means of delivery.

If there is such a thing as a legitimate bent-armer he can, when exhorted to do so, straighten his arm, or he is unworthy of the name of bowler. In passing it may be admitted that an action can degenerate through age, injury or fatigue. A case in point is that of Ramadhin, whose leg-spinner in recent years has occasionally been suspect. A reminder would, I feel certain, be sufficient to restore his arm to its original full extension.

The crux of the argument is this. *If* the 'horizontal law' is a simple and practical means of stopping an evil, which has be-devilled the game intermittently over the years, is it worthwhile rejecting it for a small minority who give nothing to the game if they in fact exist?

It has also been said that it is not always possible to see the bent arm. If this is so it also rules out the existing definition of a throw, for, as I have said, where the bend is undetectable the sudden straightening must also be so. It has been my experience that the bend has always been the obvious feature of the thrower's action, but that the straightening is very hard to determine.

The horizontal is the latest point in the swing to which full extension can safely be delayed. This is so because beyond that point the bend of the arm is a material advantage, and the difference between a bowl and a throw becomes eroded to a fine margin where recognition becomes almost impossible. In practice the vast majority of orthodox bowlers start the swing with an extended arm from a point at least forty-five degrees below this level. The only genuinely fast bowler I can recall who delayed the full extension until the horizontal was Mc-Donald, whose action, although a model of fairness, was in several respects a law unto itself. In the case of most of the great bowlers the swing has been a full straight-armed sweep, the straightening of the arm being completed somewhere just after the downward perpendicular on the final swing. O'Reilly, the greatest spinner since Barnes, had an ungainly action to look at, but the most essential part of it, the wheel of the right arm, was completely perfect, rhythmical and full, the arm straight to the utmost extension from well below the horizontal until the follow-through. It was largely this which gave him such accuracy of control over such a wide range of variation in pace, flight and spin.

To reflect on the great bowlers endorses the view that to ask a bowler to keep his arm straight is not to inflict any hardship upon him, and quite the contrary is the case in the training of the young.

The reader who has followed these arguments will appreciate they are based on a principle which differs almost diametrically from that upon which the present legislation is framed. It is that the logical approach to this problem is to provide a clear-cut definition of what constitutes a bowl as laid down by the law and to disqualify all who, for any reason, cannot comply with it. This I maintain can be done without injustice to any legitimate bowler. Further I believe that the definition suggested fulfils the requirements of clarity, precision and ease of interpretation. These claims I have more than once admitted can only be proved or disproved by practical trial, but, as I have yet to encounter any convincing rebuttal in theory, I believe that they are worth putting to the test of practical trial.

The official line has been to define a throw, or to say what must not be done and to provide for the anomalies which must arise therefrom, a very wide field indeed. Provided that this is the better approach it strikes the immediate snag of the difficulty of defining a throw in precise yet comprehensive terms. So far this has eluded a large body of intelligent, hard-thinking and experienced men. The threat of a further clause to cover extended elbow joints causes several equally thoughtful observers some alarm as to what intricacy the final formula might achieve.

The present position cannot be regarded as satisfactory. All credit to those who by courage and industry have greatly diminished the incidence of throwing, if chiefly by weight of effort. But it could recur and if it does it cannot be right that the interpretation of a rule in a game calls for film units and committee meetings deliberating far from the scene of the event in terms of time and space.

I have set out the case, I hope fairly, and it is left to the reader to say whether there is any justification for experimenting with the definition of a bowl as set out.

M.C.C. Committee Report

It is fair to say that the efforts of the ruling bodies did have a discouraging effect upon the cult of throwing. This was especially so in England and Australia, where the situation was much improved when compared with the epidemic which had afflicted the fifties. It was apparent that this was chiefly due to the efforts of selectors and umpires, for the law was still uncertain. The definition of a throw did little to clarify the situation, for in its complexity it was extremely difficult to interpret within the very limited time allowed the umpire. It was, in fact, the change of climate brought about by the authorities concerned which achieved their end, as far as this was true, rather than any clearly defined instruction regarding the technicalities involved.

There remained a number of suspects, some of whom, like Griffin and Meckiff, were condemned, but several, like Griffith and Rhodes, to whom it seemed impossible to apply the current definition of a throw, whilst actually in operation, remained in doubt. Griffith was the subject of much complaint but infrequent action, but Rhodes was a case which caused much vexation to all, not least the bowler himself.

As the general situation was clearly unresolved, the M.C.C. re-marshalled its forces and in 1965 a special committee was set up further to examine the whole question. It was under the chairmanship of F. G. Mann, and was composed of eight other

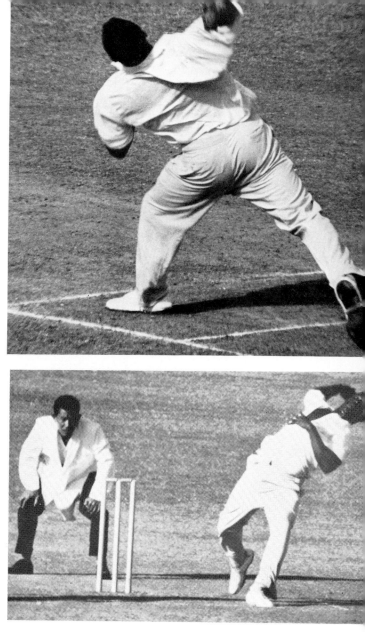

C. C. Griffith. This is surely the most extraordinary position achieved by any bowler. Again, every symptom of a throw is present to an unmistakable degree. The adjoining picture shows exactly the same characteristics seen from another viewpoint. These pictures were taken during his controversial series against Australia in the West Indies, 1965.

C. C. Griffith. This picture, taken during the West Indies tour of England in 1963, apart from the foot fault, shows an impeccable approach. The unstrained position of the torso is in strong contrast to that shown in other pictures.

OPPOSITE **H. Larwood. The start of the model final swing.** From the perfect position seen in the picture, Larwood's arm swung at full extension through an immense arc, his whole body contributing to the final heave, with chest, back and shoulders in complete unison.

The pitcher demonstrates that it is quite possible to throw from a classic sideways start.

members, each of some distinction in his particular field. They were G. O. Allen, T. E. Bailey, E. R. Dexter, C. S. Elliott, D. J. Insole, W. F. Price, R. Subba Row and R. H. Twining. Thus, players, administrators, legislators and umpires were all represented. There was no lawyer but, in times of need, the Committee could consult Mr. W. E. Tucker on the problems of anatomy.

The Committee did its work thoroughly and conscientiously and in March 1966 published a report on the results of its deliberations. It is a fairly lengthy document, but necessary reading to anyone interested in the subject. It reads as follows:

Terms of Reference

The Sub-Committee was instructed to look into further ways and means of eliminating suspect bowling actions from all grades of cricket in the United Kingdom.

The Committee's Approach to the Problem

The Committee recognised that their main objectives were:
(A) The elimination of throwing from First-Class cricket as fairly and as quickly as possible.
(B) Its elimination from other grades of cricket in the United Kingdom.
(C) As a means of achieving these two main objectives, it was considered essential to produce an improved definition, which would assist umpires in all grades of cricket in the uniform interpretation of the Law. It was appreciated that any recommended definition must be one which would be acceptable to all members of the International Cricket Conference.

(A) First-Class Cricket

(*I*) *Present Situation*

The Sub-Committee considered that the existing system, whereby an umpire 'called' a bowler when satisfied that the ball had been 'thrown', and had to submit a report on the actions of all bowlers after each match, had helped considerably in producing a clearer picture of the Umpire's opinions on the fairness or otherwise of bowlers in County Cricket. It was thought that, in the long run, this system might have the desired effect of eliminating suspect bowlers from the First-Class game. The Captains' reports had also helped to clarify the position.

Nevertheless, it was felt that this system had not proved entirely satisfactory for the following main reasons:

(a) Judging from reports received from Umpires and Captains and from the viewing of a number of films, it was evident that there were still bowlers with suspect actions.

(b) The difficulty the Umpire has in making an accurate judgment due to:

    (i) The speed of the bowler's arm in the delivery swing.

    (ii) The variation in the action of bowlers considered to be suspect.

    (iii) The position in which he normally stands at square-leg, which is not always ideal.

(c) The additional difficulty facing an umpire because of his understandable reluctance to become involved in unpleasant incidents or publicity.

(d) As a result of the above difficulties, there has been a wide variation in the opinion expressed and the action taken by umpires.

(e) In some cases, only a limited number of umpires have been sufficiently doubtful about a bowler's action to 'report' him, or confident enough of their opinion to 'call' him. In these circumstances, Counties have continued to play bowlers who may have been throwing consistently.

(*II*) *Other Factors Considered by the Committee*

(a) The Committee viewed a large number of films which convinced them of their value and necessity, as they showed far more clearly than the naked eye the details of a bowler's action. They would always be of assistance and in some cases could be an essential aid in forming a firm opinion.

(b) The desirability of giving some assistance to the umpires in the present situation was considered. The view was expressed by both Mr. Elliott and Mr. Price that all the First-Class Umpires would welcome support and assistance from an outside body. This would be particularly appreciated if, as a result of their 'calling' or 'reporting' a player, some form of sanction could be imposed. These views were supported unanimously by the Committee.

(*III*) *Recommendations*

It was recommended that:

(1) The existing system of 'calling' and 'reporting' shall continue.

(2) In addition, a Special Sub-Committee shall be set up to adjudicate on bowlers who have been 'called' or 'reported', which shall have the power to suspend a player from bowling until the end of a season.

The composition and procedure of the Committee be as follows:

(a) The following members be invited to form the Committee:

F. G. Mann (chairman); G. O. Allen (vice-chairman); F. S. Lee and J. H. Parks (retired umpires); D. J. Insole and A. V. Bedser (Board of Control selectors); T. E. Bailey, D. B. Close, M. J. K. Smith and O. S. Wheatley (current players); L. E. G. Ames and R. T. Simpson (county representatives). It was appreciated that this Committee was rather large, but it was felt that attendance during the summer, when a meeting might be called at short notice, could prove difficult.

(b) The minimum number of members required to form a quorum when adjudicating on any bowler shall be seven. Included in this number shall be:

Chairman or Vice-Chairman,

One retired umpire,

Three from the list of B.O.C. Selectors, Current Players and County Representatives.

(c) Before the Committee decide to suspend a bowler, at least two-thirds of those present shall have shown to be in favour of suspension. Should a member of the Committee be connected with the County of the bowler concerned, he should have no vote, nor be counted as present for the purpose of calculating the voting percentage.

(d)   The following procedure should be adopted:

    (i)   After one report by an umpire or a captain, or on the recommendation of a member of the Committee, the player shall be filmed in black and white in at least two matches from varying angles and at varying speeds, including slow motion. Members of the Committee will also watch him, if possible.

   (ii)   After two reports by umpires, the Committee shall adjudicate on a bowler's action, though they should have power to do this after only one report, if they so wished.

  (iii)   Having decided that a bowler's basic action is unfair, the Committee shall have power to suspend him from bowling until the end of the season.

  (iv)   The Committee might, at their discretion, following four reports by umpires on one bowler, suspend him immediately until such time as they have the opportunity of adjudicating.

   (v)   In cases where the Committee 'clear' a bowler's basic action, but regard him as an occasional 'thrower', it is intended that they shall, at their discretion, make whatever additional comments they may think proper for the assistance of umpires in the light of the evidence they have seen and heard.

  (vi)   In the cases where the Committee completely clear a bowler, the County Committee and umpires concerned will be notified accordingly. At the same time it will be pointed out that this clearance does not preclude umpires from 'calling' or 'reporting' the bowler in the future.

 (vii)   In 1966 and in subsequent seasons bowlers shall start with a 'clean sheet' unless a County make a particular request for adjudication before the commencement of the season.

(viii)   The County concerned in a particular case

shall be entitled to express its views to the Committee if it wishes to do so.

(3) Prior to the 1966 season, a special meeting of the First-Class Umpires shall be held at Lord's, at which the machinery of the new Committee will be explained. The umpires will also be invited to view films of both fair and suspect bowlers, but in the latter category they shall be players who have retired from First-Class Cricket.

(B) Other Grades of Cricket

Undoubtedly there are throwers in other grades of cricket and steps shall be taken to move towards their elimination.

The Committee make the following recommendations:

(i) *Minor County Umpires*
That the Minor County Umpires, as with the First-Class Umpires, be invited to Lord's at the beginning of the coming season, for a discussion and to view films.

(ii) *Umpires In Other Grades of Cricket*
That steps be taken to contact the Association of Cricket Umpires and the Yorkshire Federation of Cricket Umpires, to seek their advice and co-operation. Firm proposals will be made later.

(iii) *Coaches and Players*
That a new film on bowling shall be produced, which will be concerned principally with instruction of the correct bowling action. It shall, however, include some examples of 'suspect' actions and shall point out the 'danger signs' of which a coach shall take particular notice and correct before it is too late.

(C) Definition of a Throw

(I) Present Situation in the United Kingdom

The existing definition which exists in all countries at the present time, and should, in the opinion of the Sub-Committee, continue to be used in this country until the International Cricket Conference decides otherwise, reads as follows:

'A ball shall be deemed to have been thrown if, in the opinion of either Umpire, the bowling arm, having been bent at the elbow, whether the wrist is backward of the elbow or not, is suddenly straightened immediately prior to the instant of delivery. The bowler shall nevertheless be at liberty to use the wrist freely in the delivery action.'

(*II*) *Views of the International Cricket Conference*

Following a discussion at the last meeting of the International Cricket Conference, the delegates recommended the following definition for consideration by their respective Boards:

'A ball shall be deemed to have been thrown if, in the opinion of either Umpire, the bowling arm is straightened, whether partially or completely, immediately prior to the ball leaving the hand. This definition shall not debar the bowler from the use of the wrist in delivering the ball.'

Most countries have accepted the above proposal, but Australia have not supported it, since they consider that the words 'immediately prior to . . .' are open to doubt in interpretation and that there appears to be a body of opinion in some countries who have maintained that, under the existing definition, which also includes these words, a bowler is 'fair', provided his arm is straight at the instant of delivery. The Committee believe that there is some substance in Australia's objection.

(*III*) *Other Factors Considered by the Committee*

When considering alternative definitions, the Committee have borne in mind that bowlers who contravene the Law vary in their methods, in that they straighten their arms in different ways and start to do so at different points in their delivery swings. They are, nevertheless, convinced that, for a bowler to 'throw', the arm must be in the process of straightening during the final stages of the delivery swing, i.e. in the 50 degrees to 60 degrees before the ball leaves the hand, though, of course, some bowlers begin to straighten well before this point.

During their deliberations the Committee considered the possibility of defining a fair delivery based on the bowler maintaining a fully extended arm from the horizontal until the ball leaves the hand. In spite of its apparent simplicity of interpretation, this suggestion is not supported for the reasons stated in the previous paragraph and for the fact that, although such a definition might be slightly easier to interpret, umpires would still have the difficulty of judging whether or not a bowler's arm was bent in the latter part of the delivery swing. The Committee decided that any recommended definition should be clear to interpret, should, if possible, overcome the objections raised by Australia and should be fair to the bowlers. They feel that any definition designed to catch the 'guilty', but capable of penalising the 'innocent' should be avoided.

(IV) Recommendation

It was recommended that the following definition be submitted to the International Cricket Conference in July, 1966:

'A ball shall be deemed to have been thrown if, in the opinion of either umpire, the process of straightening the bowling arm, whether it be partial or complete, takes place during that part of the delivery swing which directly precedes the ball leaving the hand. This definition shall not debar the bowler from the use of the wrist in delivering the ball.'

The reasons for this recommendation are:

(a) The sole objection to the definition recommended by the International Cricket Conference in 1965 has been that the words 'immediately prior to . . .' could be taken to mean that if a bowler's arm is straight at the instant of delivery, the ball is fair.

(b) In the recommended definition above the Committee believes that this possible misinterpretation has been precluded by the introduction of the following words: 'the process of straightening the bowling arm' and 'takes place during that part of the delivery swing which directly precedes . . .'

*   *   *

Despite its thorough and comprehensive nature the report did not reach the real root of the problem.

To many people it seemed desirable that the laws of cricket should be capable of clear and final interpretation by the umpire on the spot. The general trend of the report was in the opposite direction. In calling a bowler for infringing laws the umpire was to set in motion a complicated trend of events far removed from the actual scene.

The existing situation, as reviewed in the report, had been sufficiently burdensome in practice, but to this was now added the paraphernalia of committees, films, and all the attendant machinery.

The final Section (c) provides the most interesting reading, for here the report grapples with what is obviously the crux of the whole matter. For if the definition of a throw could be clarified to the point where there could be no doubt as to what constituted an infringement of the law there would be no necessity for the elephantine procedure outlined in the body of the report. Ideally, an offending bowler would be called for his immediate performance without regard to his reputation, which would be established, one way or another, on the firm ground of the umpire's decision. Thereafter all that would be necessary would be to introduce a factor calculated to make such infringement so unprofitable to the bowler, and his team, that the basically unsuitable action would be unsaleable, and the occasional offender careful to desist.

At present the penalty for a throw is one run, debited to extras. If a fielder defies his code by stopping the ball otherwise than 'with any part of his person' the penalty is much heavier— five runs, credited to the batsman, if the ball has been struck (and debited to an unoffending bowler). Why not on this precedent make the penalty for throwing a really stiff imposition, say ten or twenty runs, to be added to the bowling analysis of the culprit? This would, incidentally, prove a useful deterrent to the fast bowler who might consider one extra a small price to pay for the alarm and uncertainty to be gained from the occasional bouncer of sudden and unexpected venom.

However, Section (c) furthers the tacit admission that the definition of a throw, even in its amended form, cannot provide a dependable basis for a clear decision. So long as this is the case, it is probable that the matter will be subject to the remote control of camera or committee, and the umpire's role reduced to that of observer and informant.

Elsewhere I have set out the reasons why I believe that the only way to bring about a workable situation is to define a bowl, rather than a throw. This I have done because it seems to me to be possible to achieve the first object with a brevity and lucidity which has so far eluded all attempts to describe a throw with any precision, and in all probability will continue to do so.

In sub-section (iii) of Section (c), 'Definition of a Throw', the report says:

When considering alternative definitions the Committee have borne in mind that the bowlers who contravene the law vary in their methods, in that they straighten their arms in different ways and start to do so at different points in their delivery swings. They are nevertheless convinced that to 'throw' the arm must be in the process of straightening during the final stages of the delivery swing, i.e. in the 50 degrees to 60 degrees before the ball leaves the hand, though, of course, some bowlers begin to straighten well before this point.

During their deliberations, the Committee considered the possibility of defining a fair delivery based on the bowler maintaining a fully extended arm from the horizontal until the ball leaves the hand. In spite of its apparent simplicity of interpretation, this suggestion was not supported for the reasons stated in the previous paragraph and for the fact that, although such a definition might be slightly easier to interpret, umpires would still have the difficulty of judging whether or not a bowler's arm was bent in the latter part of the delivery swing. The Committee decided that any recommended definition should be clear to interpret, should, if possible, overcome objections raised by Australia and should be fair to the bowlers. They feel that any definition designed to catch the 'guilty', but capable of penalising the 'innocent', should be avoided.

The first of the above paragraphs is clear enough, bearing in mind that in order to straighten the arm it must be initially bent. It is the second paragraph which, in citing the contents

G

of its predecessor as grounds for rejecting the 'extended arm' definition, so completely confuses the issue. Surely 'the previous paragraph' sets out the strongest case for a clear-cut definition of a bowl which would exclude all the variations attributed to those who contravene the law. If the bowler is required to extend his arm above the horizontal the legislator need not concern himself with any of the aforesaid complications. He merely has to apply himself to the most discernible part of the whole operation, the bend of the arm, and that within a clearly defined area. The report's statement that 'such a definition might be slightly easier to interpret but the umpire would still have the difficulty of judging whether or not a bowler's arm was bent in the latter part of the swing' is irrefutable but baffling. It *would* be a difficulty, but this is something the umpire has to surmount in varying degree when arriving at almost every decision he is called upon to make. Compared with the complications he is expected to master in applying the definition of a throw, it is purely a trivial one. All the other factors in paragraph A (1) of the report pertaining to the speed of the bowler's arm, the varieties of action, and the position of the umpire also apply, to the man looking for a bend above the horizontal; but to an infinitely lesser degree than to one trying to discern 'a sudden straightening partial or complete' in a period described as that which 'directly precedes the ball leaving the hand'.

Once again, the plea is made that the innocent should be safeguarded, a very proper consideration. But just what is the connotation of the word 'innocent'? If it is our old friend the 'legitimate' bent-arm bowler I still deny his existence. Under the suggestion of a bowling definition he has but to extend his arm as every orthodox bowler is required to do. But if the bent arm is to be tolerated it makes the 'throwing' definition impossible of practical application, unless the observer has the eye of a slow-motion camera. If the Committee genuinely believe that the extended arm is more readily interpretable it is astonishing that they should let such a nebulous objection prevent its practical trial. The fact remains that when an easily workable definition of a bowl *or a throw* is proved in practice a very controversial problem will be resolved. Each incident will then be summarily and finally dealt with when and where it ought to be, on the field by the proper authority, who is the officiating umpire.

At the moment of writing there has been a suggestion that it will be necessary to introduce a further clause to cover the case of a bowler who has an extension of the elbow joint. This has no doubt arisen from the case of Rhodes, whose arm bends backward some degrees beyond the normal straight line. Some observers aver that in his delivery swing Rhodes' arm swings forward to the straight or beyond it. This may well be so, but it is difficult to see what the extension has to do with this particular movement. Any normal arm can be subject to the same forces and it would seem to be irrelevant whether the forearm swings forward from a straight line or a point ten degrees beyond it. Technically either would infringe the 'horizontal law', although I doubt if a small degree of flexion would be perceptible or have any material effect. It is, however, perfectly possible for any man with a normal, or an abnormal, freedom of the elbow joint to keep his arm fully extended for the operative part of the delivery swing. Perhaps I may be allowed to say that I have some immediate knowledge of this matter, having myself some extension of the elbow joint.

It is to be hoped that this suggestion will not be accepted for it would add further confusion to an already blurred and complicated scene.

A final point—it is surely desirable that there should be complete uniformity of procedure not only in all grades of cricket but in all cricket-playing countries. In England any system approximating to that laid down for first-class cricket would be extremely difficult to apply to club cricket. This the Committee obviously recognises, as will be seen from (B) 'Other Grades of Cricket'. The report promises that 'firm proposals will be made later'. It is unlikely that these proposals will advocate anything as elaborate as the machinery for first-class cricket, so one must assume that there will be a considerable divergence in practical application. To judge from the proposals for the Minor Counties and the consultation to be held with the representative bodies of umpires, the trend will be to leave the major responsibility with the umpire. This would be at variance with the policy laid down for the senior grade.

Whether other members of the International Cricket Conference will want to model their procedure on the English lines remains to be seen. It is doubtful if in several of the countries the system could be implemented, whatever the views of the ruling body concerned.

At the moment of writing the case of M. E. Scott, the Northamptonshire left-hander, has come under the scrutiny of the Committee. It does not strike one as a very happy precedent, for here is a bowler who has been suspended from cricket without having been called by any umpire. Commenting upon this, E. W. Swanton remarked in the *Daily Telegraph* that this savoured too much of the Star Chamber to be approved by most cricketers. It would surely have been a less unhappy situation had the umpire on the spot been able to decide whether or not Scott had infringed the law.

The Case for Legalising Throwing

In January of 1897 F. R. Spofforth, generally considered to be the greatest bowler the world had yet seen, publicly joined the prevailing controversy on unfair bowling. In a letter addressed to the editor of *Sporting Life* he set forth his views and put forward his own suggestion for the solution of the problem. It was a surprising one. The relevant part of his letter read:

> But what I consider a far more serious consideration for the authorities is, are they going to legalise throwing? There is scarcely a first class county which does not include a 'thrower' amongst its cricketers, many of them men who would scorn to cheat an opponent out, and who, if a wicket-keeper were in the habit of kicking down the stumps or knocking off the bails with his hands and appealing for a bowl out, would not hesitate to bring him before his committee, or refuse to play with him again. Still, they will not only employ a man to throw, but will actually throw themselves, and acknowledge it, their only excuse being that 'others do it', and they will name many.
>
> This practice of throwing is growing rapidly, and many young cricketers are now adopting it who a year or so back were quite above suspicion.
>
> Australia has now taken it up, and with the last eleven there was one who hardly ever delivered a 'fair' ball, and although I am quite aware I may raise a 'hornet's nest' about my head for mentioning names, I allude to McKibbin who, I shall always maintain, should never be allowed to play under the existing rule.

Now, I think it is only fair I should mention an Englishman, and although I could name many I am anxious not to injure anyone. So I will take Bobby Peel, one of England's best bowlers, and one who has no need to resort to throwing. I acknowledge he does not often take to it, still it is well known to cricketers that at times he does 'shy'. Again, there are many who, while not exactly throwing do not bowl fairly according to the existing rule. They 'put' the ball, which is they throw only from one point, mostly the elbow. The remedy for this unfair play is rather hard to find, especially as there is no umpire in England who dare no-ball a cricketer, while should a fair bowler even touch the bowler's crease when delivering a ball he is at once 'called'.

I am of opinion the best way to put down throwing is to form a committee of all the captains of the first class counties with Lord Harris as chairman, and on anyone being reported for throwing, a vote to be taken, and if unfavourable the cricketer be suspended for a week, if brought up a second time fined and suspended, a third time he should be disqualified for the season. Both jockeys and footballers are suspended and fined for unfairness, and why should cricketers be exempt?

In conclusion, if nothing is to be done in the matter, the best way is to legalise throwing, and in one season it would bring about its own cure.

Yours etc.

January 25, 1897   Fred R. Spofforth

Spofforth was not only a great bowler but a profound student of every aspect of his craft, and a man of penetrating intelligence. He must also have been aware of the great respect with which his views would be received. In this instance, however, one wonders whether he had thought the question out to its final implications or whether he spoke impulsively in his affront at the despoiling of an art which he had done so much to develop.

He drew a rejoinder from A. G. Steel, another much respected authority on this subject, who, writing in *Wisden* of 1900, says:

I have heard irresponsible people and even some others suggest that throwing should be legalised, the argument being that on the good wickets common nowadays, it would not in any way jeopardize the batsman's safety. That may be so; I daresay that on absolutely perfect wickets there would be no danger. I refer to such a wicket as was played on in the England v. Australia match at the Oval last August—a wicket so carefully prepared that though fast and true it was utterly devoid of all life and elasticity, and on which the fastest bowler could not make the ball rise above half stump high. In all probability on this class of wicket the best and fastest throwers would not appreciably lower the scoring. But take a crumbled wicket for instance, or a hard wicket after a shower heavy enough to soften it say a quarter of an inch only. What would happen then? I have never had the pleasure of playing Jones the Australian, but I have seen him bowl on one or two funny wickets and though probably a real first-class batsman would not whilst batting appreciate that there was any danger owing to his quickness and agility, to an onlooker he seemed decidedly 'awkward'. Now if Jones—a recognised fair bowler—could do this, what would a recognised thrower do?

As the strong action taken by certain umpires, supported by M.C.C. and the county captains, eradicated most of the unsatisfactory bowlers within the following two or three years the suggestion of legalised throwing faded and never came to much prominence during the following comparatively peaceful half-century.

When the controversy arose again after the events of May's Australian tour the cry for legalised throwing was heard again, but, this time, unsupported by any prominent player, past or present. However, J. L. Manning, writing in the *Daily Mail* in June 1965, on the vexed case of Rhodes, said:

In two weeks' time the Imperial Cricket Conference will ask M.C.C. to prepare a new definition of throwing. It will waste time and invest the game with more controversy. In 1828, G. T. Knight, a member of M.C.C., wrote: 'There is no need to define throwing; you might as well try to define the action of the horse trotting.'

That still holds good in 1965. If there is one clear conclusion to be drawn from the judgment of Buller at Derbyshire assizes it is clear that everyone thinks he knows the difference between bowling and throwing, yet no one can say what it is.

It is time to sweep aside confusion and reticence, and put the facts before a bewildered and suspicious cricket public.

The facts known about the bowling of Harold Rhodes add up to an astonishing situation.

Between August 8, 1961, when Umpire Gibb no-balled Rhodes three times in succession against Northamptonshire, and Monday, when Umpire Buller twice called him in South Africa's first match, the following events took place:

1. D. B. Carr, then his captain and now M.C.C. assistant secretary, put him on the other end and Umpire Jepson passed him.

2. Umpire Gibb passed him at the Oval 11 days later when he bowled 246 deliveries.

3. He bowled 15,191 deliveries in the next three-and-a-half years without any umpire calling him.

4. During that time 29 different English umpires stood in his matches, including Gibb, the original caller (six times), Buller, his latest caller (three times), and Pepper, who wanted to call Griffith (four times). None called him.

5. Rhodes's action this season was filmed for his county club at Buxton and for M.C.C. at Lord's. Only as a result of the Lord's film, over which there seems to be some mystery, did the chairman of selectors write to Derbyshire. He then said Rhodes's action was so doubtful that he could not be considered for Tests.

At that time he had bowled about 1,800 balls this season, was top of the averages and had not been called by any umpire under the new definition of a throw. There were, however, complaints from opponents.

Nevertheless it is asking too much from the public to believe Buller's action this week, five days before an England team is announced, was coincidence.

It is true that during all the bowling Rhodes has done un-challenged on the field, the definition of throwing has been expanded. But I cannot accept that Rhodes suddenly reverted to throwing after three-and-a-half years, and that Buller suddenly spotted it while his colleague at the other end did not.

The facts are overwhelmingly against this being the true position, and a majority of the public, in my view, will not accept it.

I will tell you why these difficulties occur. Bowling is an unnatural action. No one aiming a ball at the wicket would 'bowl'. He would throw.

Lapses into throwing, therefore, are natural. What is happening now is that bowling is evolving a new phase, just as it changed from under-arm to round-arm and from round-arm to over-arm to meet the challenge of batting techniques.

This bowling evolution was as bitterly and violently resisted in the past as it is now. Throwing is not itself a danger, as thousands of runs scored off it in recent years have shown.

Near-as-damn-it throwing, like any bowling, is dangerous only when it is intimidatory and its target is the batsman not his wicket.

These are the lines on which lawmakers of the future must work. It is not possible to define with brevity and clarity in an enforceable law the distinction between purity of bowling and imperfection of a throw.

Umpires are always left with the dilemma that precise definition at once legalises the slightest variation not specifically prohibited.

I am told this will turn cricket into baseball. The present difficulty is to turn cricket into cricket.

Be in no doubt. The 'throwing' bowler has come to stay, just as the over-arm bowler did 101 years ago. It will do no harm if the batsman is properly protected by cricket's other laws.

Besides, the modern batsman has asked for all he is getting.

Anyone who has read this book thus far will be aware that I share Mr. Manning's doubts as to the possibility of defining a throw. There are few other points in the general advocacy of legalising throwing which bear close examination.

To dispose of one, bowling is not an unnatural action, as any toddler will demonstrate. It is one which is seldom developed outside its requirements for cricket, whereas a throw which is more or less unnatural is the easier and more convenient form of propulsion for a wide range of purposes from exercising a dog to assaulting a public speaker, where a run-up is not available. Thus throwing is much more widely practised.

To lapse into throwing is neither natural nor necessary to anyone properly trained to bowl. Certainly cases of orthodox bowlers *becoming* chuckers are very rare. And throwing is not the natural and logical evolution of the progression from underhand to round-arm and thence to over-arm bowling, which all have a common derivation. It is an entirely different class of movement. The whole basis of the arguments I have set out is that, whilst it is impossible to define a throw it *is* possible to produce, 'with brevity and clarity in an enforceable law the distinction between purity of bowling and imperfection of a throw'. This to my mind is perfectly practicable by defining a bowl in the terms I have quoted and allowing no exception to them.

If the solution to the whole problem was to legalise throwing the result would not be baseball, a game with special merits of its own, but bastard ball, which could have very few. The batsmen would require a rather more material form of protection than the mere laws could afford.

Surely the first objection to the introduction of the pitcher, as opposed to the bowler, into cricket, is that envisaged by A. G. Steel almost seventy years ago. In considering the question of the safety of the batsman there is a very important factor which may have escaped the notice of protagonists of the free-for-all movement.

I have endeavoured to show that the illegal bowler's action is that of the javelin thrower, as this movement is, up to a point, similar to the bowler's preliminary movement and readily adaptable to his main delivery. As has been seen in practice, it affords a considerable advantage and, its application being a matter of degrees, not always easy to discern.

Were all restraint to be removed it is not the halfway house between bowl and throw which would be favoured but the full-blooded hurl of the outfielder or baseball pitcher. This has not yet been seen in cricket, for, as I have argued, it is so far removed from *any* form of bowling that it would be instantly recognised and suppressed.

The expert pitcher is reckoned to generate the pace of the fastest bowler. But this is from the safeguard of a standing start, and calls for the additional effort of propelling the ball full toss, or on the fly, a distance of twenty yards, to arrive above the knee level of the striker. If the pitcher were allowed to run up, gather himself, and dig the ball in at twelve yards' range, I imagine the result would make any bowler, legitimate or otherwise, look comparatively tame.

On the most perfect pitches this would pose problems to the most accomplished batsman. On worn or faulty wickets it would be highly dangerous, and in club cricket these dangers would be emphasised. Village cricket would be mayhem, for a good strong arm could soon achieve a pace which only a very skilful and long-trained bowler could rival and, despite legendary tales of village blacksmiths, real pace is very rare outside first-class cricket, and something with which the unpractised striker just cannot cope.

It would therefore be necessary to take radical measures for the protection of the striker in all grades of cricket. In considering such measures it must be borne in mind that the batsman is in a very different position from the baseball batter. The latter is unconcerned with length and bounce, so is most advantageously placed at the length of arm and the most responsive part of the club from the line of the ball—at which he swings in a flat plane. The essence of almost every cricket stroke, apart from the cut, is to be right up to the line of the ball, the batsman accepting the occasionally painful consequences of his own misjudgment. For this contingency he is under present circumstances adequately protected, although there remains the possibility of severe injury in the event of an accident. In order to guard against the sharply increased risk of such injury, and its most serious consequences, it would be necessary to give the batsman a much greater degree of physical protection. This would entail comprehensive body armour and face mask and, in all probability, a crash helmet. The inconvenience and discomfort, even in an age of lightweight plastics, would hardly be conducive to free stroke-play, but this would, in any case, be greatly restricted by sheer speed and the lack of that anticipation afforded by the orthodox bowling action. The expense would be a considerable item in the budgets of smaller clubs.

It would, of course, be possible to lengthen the pitch at the expense of spin whether bowled or thrown, but, again, this would doubtless be a minor consideration in any case.

A third alternative would be to make the pitcher operate from a standing start as his baseball counterpart. This would finally rule out any question of bowling.

Whichever course might be adopted the influence on batting would be profound. The free-swinging strokes which are the basis of classical play would be severely curtailed. Batsmen who have had experience of the 'chucker' complain of the difficulty of making strokes because of the impossibility of judging pace or direction from the quick, flipping aim of the pitcher as against the rhythmical swing of the bowler. This, combined with sheer pace, would confine batting to prodding pushes and deflections.

One conclusion which arises again in the study of this subject, against the game as a whole, is that the laws of cricket, applied in their accepted spirit, are remarkably adequate. In general, the less they are amended the better. The point I have striven to make is that in one particular aspect they call for clarification.

Principal instances of bowlers no-balled for throwing in first-class cricket

J. WILLES **Fast round-arm**
Kent v. M.C.C.
Lord's. July 15, 16, 1822

This is the first officially recorded case of a man being no-balled for his action. Until 1810 a 'no ball' only applied to foot-faults. In 1810 M.C.C. introduced the first clause governing action. It read: 'The ball is to be bowled underhand, and delivered with the hand below the elbow.'

As this was ineffective an amendment was made in 1816 to read: 'The ball must be bowled (not thrown or jerked) and be delivered underhand with the hand below the elbow, but if the ball be jerked or the arm extended below the elbow, or the arm extended from the body horizontally when the ball is delivered, the umpire shall call "No ball".'

It was under this ruling that Willes was no-balled by Noah Mann for raising his arm above the prescribed level. (According to some accounts he was called by H. Bentley, the other umpire, but H. S. Altham, a most reliable authority, settles for Noah Mann).

E. WILLSHER **Fast left-hand**
England v. Surrey
The Oval. August 25, 26, 27, 1862

Willsher was no-balled seven times in succession by John Lillywhite. All nine England professionals left the field and the game was only resumed on the following day when another umpire was substituted for Lillywhite. Willsher was disqualified for raising his arm above the round-arm level, legalised in 1835.

G. E. JOWETT   Fast right-hand

Lancashire v. Surrey
Liverpool. July 16, 17, 18, 1885

Jowett played for Lancashire between 1885 and 1889. Despite the presence of Crossland, Nash and Watson, he was the only bowler actually called. J. Platts was the umpire. Jowett was certainly the least successful of these bowlers, for in five seasons with the county he failed to take a wicket.

E. JONES   Fast right-hand

South Australia v. A. E. Stoddart's Team
Adelaide. October 28, 29, 30, November 1, 1897
Australia v. England - Second Test
Melbourne. January 1, 3, 4, 5, 1898

Jones was called on both occasions by Phillips. He played against Stoddart's team in all five Test matches and twice for South Australia. On each occasion Phillips stood umpire but raised no objection except on these two occasions. Jones' action was the subject of some adverse criticism on his visit to England in 1896, when his pace was regarded as comparable to Kortright, but was not actually called. Nor was he no-balled for throwing during the remainder of his career in first-class cricket. See text, pages **17–19**.

C. B. FRY   Fast-medium right-hand

Sussex v. Nottinghamshire
Trent Bridge. June 16, 17, 18, 1898
Umpire: West

Sussex v. Oxford University
Hove. June 23, 24, 25, 1898
Umpire: Phillips

Sussex v. Middlesex
Lord's. July 14, 15, 16, 1898
Umpire: Sherwin

Fry had for some years been prominent amongst a number of suspected bowlers. Sydney Pardon, editor of *Wisden,* had been equally prominent in leading a campaign against what he considered a grave malpractice. In the issue for 1899 he delivered a manifesto with particular reference to Fry:

THROWING
A Note by the Editor

A twelvemonth ago I ventured to say nothing but good could come from James Phillips's action in no-balling Jones, the Australian fast bowler, for throwing. I did not imagine, however, that the result would be either so speedy or so satisfactory. Throwing on English cricket grounds had for such a long time been allowed to go unchecked—the umpires taking no heed of even the most flagrant offenders—that I was not prepared to see any steps taken last season. When once a man has done a courageous thing, however, he is very apt to find imitators, and such was James Phillips's case last season. For the first time within my experience—with one trifling exception—bowlers were no-balled in first-class matches in England for throwing, Mr. C. B. Fry being no-balled by West at Trent Bridge, by Phillips himself at Brighton and by Sherwin at Lord's; and the new Warwickshire bowler, Hopkins, coming under the ban of Titchmarsh at Tonbridge. More than that there were, I believe, one or two cases of no-balling in matches played by the smaller counties. The no-balling of Mr. Fry was only a case of long-delayed justice. As a matter of fact he ought never, after his caricature of bowling in the M.C.C. and Oxford match at Lord's in 1892, to have been allowed to bowl at all. As he had enjoyed immunity for six years I cannot regard him as an object of sympathy, but he could fairly urge that during that time many bowlers far more formidable than he had been permitted to throw without protest. However, in nearly all cases of reform someone has to suffer and so far from Mr. Fry's fame as a cricketer declining, he proceeded as soon as he gave up bowling to bat as he had never batted before. Personally, I

88APPENDIX I

regard the no-balling of Hopkins as even more significant than that of
Mr. Fry. While the latter might be looked upon as an old offender,
Hopkins was a new man, just at the outset of his career. In this point lay
the importance of what Titchmarsh did at Tonbridge. Let it once be
understood that new bowlers who do not deliver the ball with strict fairness will be no-balled, and throwing will strictly disappear from first-class
cricket. To the contention that it is difficult for umpires to distinguish
between throwing and fair bowling I have never attached the slightest
importance. An umpire who is fit for his post can always tell and, moreover, it is important to bear in mind that a rule was specially framed to
help him, Law 48A reading: 'If the umpire at the bowler's end be not
satisfied of the absolute fairness of the delivery of any ball, he shall call
"no ball".' Inasmuch as this rule deprives the offender of the benefit of
the doubt, it may be rather dubious law, but it immensely strengthens the
hands of the umpire.

F. J. HOPKINS Slow right-hand

Warwickshire v. Kent
Tonbridge. June 20, 21, 22, 1898
Umpire: Titchmarsh

Hopkins was a young slow bowler who had met with some success
earlier in the season. It was an unfortunate occasion for him in that
he also made a 'pair'. See also above.

CAPTAIN E. R. BRADFORD Fast right-hand

Hampshire v. Australians
Southampton. August 3, 4, 5, 1899
Umpires: White and Pickett

Hampshire v. Leicestershire
Leicester. August 10, 11, 12, 1899
Umpire: Smith

Captain E. R. Bradford was one of a fine military trio who led the
Hampshire batting averages in 1899, Major Poore averaging 116,

Captain Wynyard 49, and Captain Bradford 44. Captain Bradford met with some initial success as a fast bowler, but immediate objection was taken to his action, and he was called by both umpires in the Australian match and by Smith in his next appearance at Leicester. He was compensated by a century against Leicestershire, but, ironically, was bowled by his fellow sufferer, Jones, for a duck in the Australian match. Bradford succeeded as the 2nd Baronet and, as Colonel Sir Evelyn Bradford of the Seaforth Highlanders, he was killed in action in 1914.

R. G. HARDSTAFF   Medium left-hand

Nottinghamshire v. Australians
Trent Bridge. July 3, 4, 5, 1899
Umpire: West

This was Hardstaff's last appearance for Nottinghamshire. He bowled 42 overs in taking one for 68, so it is to be surmised that he was an occasional rather than a basic offender.

C. B. FRY   Fast-medium right-hand

Sussex v. Gloucestershire
Hove. June 4, 5, 6, 1900
Umpire: West

Fry was no-balled during his first spell, but *Wisden* states that 'going on a second time he bowled with a perfectly fair action'. In Sussex's first innings Fry was bowled for nought by Paish, later himself to be called.

A. MOLD   Fast right-hand

Lancashire v. Nottinghamshire
Trent Bridge. June 25, 26, 27, 1900
Umpire: Phillips

H

This was the first time Mold had been officially challenged in a dozen years. He bowled but one over in Nottinghamshire's two completed innings. See text, pages 4–7.

E. J. TYLER   Slow left-hand

Somerset v. Surrey
Taunton. August 27, 28, 29, 1900
Umpire: Phillips

Tyler was the first slow bowler to be no-balled for throwing during this campaign. This point was duly applauded by Sydney Pardon in his notes on the season, quoted:

> I had intended to write at considerable length on the subject of unfair bowling and the no-balling of Mold and Tyler by James Phillips, but before I had started on my task the announcement appeared that at the meeting of county captains at Lord's, on December 10, an agreement had been made to take united action in the season of 1901, for the purpose of ridding English cricket of all throwing and dubious bowling. Up to the time of these lines being written—December 14—full details of the method to be employed have not been officially made public, but I am assured on the highest authority that very strong measures have been determined on. Some bowlers will not be put on at all in county matches and others will receive a significant warning. 'Better late than never', but I cannot help thinking what a number of scandals and what an immense amount of grumbling would have been avoided, if in the middle of the 'eighties', the county captains had taken concerted action. At that time, however, Lord Harris alone had the courage of his convictions, and really tried to grapple with an admitted evil. It will not be forgotten that in 1885, Kent, at Lord Harris's instigation, dropped their return match with Lancashire on the ground that the Northern county employed unfair bowlers. Things have never since been so bad as they were about that time, when on one occasion three unmistakable throwers took part in a Gentlemen v. Players' match at Lord's, but within the last few years there has un-questionably been great laxity. I think that the necessity of doing something was first brought home to the M.C.C. committee and the county authorities when Jones and McKibbin so flagrantly disregarded Law 10, during the Australian tour of 1896. Even the least observant of cricketers must have been struck by the change that had come over Australian

bowling since Spofforth, Boyle, Garrett, Palmer, Turner and Ferris earned their laurels on English cricket grounds. The mortifying fact was that the deplorable change was due entirely to our own weakness in not having the laws of the game carried out. The Australians only did against us what we had over and over again done against them. Now that at last English cricketers are taking steps to put their house in order, I think I may, without undue egotism, take some small credit to myself for having tried, year after year, to get rid of unfair bowling. I denounced Crossland as a thrower the first time he ever played at Lord's, he being then quite an unknown man; and since that time I have in various newspapers, as well as in *Wisden*, urged our cricket authorities to make a firm stand on behalf of fair bowling. To the argument that it is impossible to distinguish between throwing and legitimate bowling, I attach no importance whatever. I wonder what my old friend Bob Thoms would say if anyone told him he could not tell a throw from a fairly bowled ball. A throw may be difficult to define in words, but to the eye of a practical and unbiased cricketer it is, I think, very obvious. James Phillips holds to the opinion that when a bowler strikes one at first sight as being a thrower, the odds are a hundred to one that he is not bowling fairly. In support of his opinion there is the fact that no bowler with an unimpeachably fair action has ever been accused of throwing. I have heard hard things said of Phillips for having no-balled Jones in Australia, and C. B. Fry, Mold and Tyler in this country, but in my opinion he has done splendid service to the game of cricket. He proved to our formerly timid officials that an umpire could enforce the law without any detriment to his professional position, and his good example was quickly followed by W. A. J. West, Titchmarsh and Sherwin. As to the no-balling of Mold at Trent Bridge, and Tyler at Taunton, I can say nothing at first-hand as I was not present at either match. Mr. A. C. MacLaren defended Mold in the columns of the *Manchester Evening News*, but the defence did not really amount to much. Anyway he did not commit himself to the opinion that Mold was a strictly fair bowler. Knowing what I do as to the opinions expressed in private by several of the greatest batsmen in the country, I regard Mold as the luckiest of men to have gone through nearly a dozen seasons before being no-balled. The no-balling of Tyler was valuable in another way, as it emphasised the often neglected truth that a slow ball can be just as much a throw as a fast one.

J. J. MARSH   Fast right-hand

New South Wales v. Victoria
Melbourne. December 24, 26, 27, 1900

Marsh was an aborigine, like Gilbert of later years. He was no-balled twice by Crockett, a stern and courageous umpire. Despite this set-back Marsh had a good match, taking six wickets for 91 on the losing side. He also made a 'pair'.

J. J. MARSH   Fast right-hand
New South Wales v. Victoria
Sydney. February 1, 2, 4, 5, 1901

Crockett followed up his warning shots at Melbourne by no-balling Marsh nineteen times in the return match. Marsh finished the season with 24 wickets in Sheffield Shield games for 22.37 apiece, but this ended his career in State Cricket.

A. MOLD   Fast right-hand
Lancashire v. Somerset
Old Trafford. July 11 and 12, 1901

On the opening day Phillips no-balled Mold sixteen times and so ended his career. Mold bowled unchallenged in the second innings but did not again play in a first-class match. Appended is the full report from the *Daily Telegraph* of July 12, 1901, which provides a most interesting contemporary comment upon Mold in particular and the throwing problem in general. There are certain inconsistencies in this report, possibly due to pressure of time and events.

THROWING OR BOWLING?
MOLD NO-BALLED AT OLD TRAFFORD.
OPINIONS OF EXPERTS.

Since the M.C.C. committee deprecated the actual suspension of any bowler this season little has been heard of the throwing controversy which raged so fiercely after the drastic step determined on by the captains at their meeting in December became known, but as the result of what happened at Manchester yesterday it will now be revived in full force. To come at once to the point, James Phillips, in the Lancashire and Somerset match at Old Trafford, no-balled Mold eighteen times—first when standing at short-leg and afterwards when Mold was put on at his end. Hitherto this season the Lancashire authorities have shirked danger by not playing Mold in matches in which Phillips has been one of the umpires, but, with a desire to bring matters once for all to a head, Mr. MacLaren—with the full approval of his committee—not only included Mold in the team yesterday, but put him on at the start of the game. We think the course taken was a wise one, as, whatever difference of opinion may exist as to the fairness of Mold's action, there was something rather ignominious in Lancashire only playing him when the one umpire who had no-balled him was not officiating. Such a feeble compromise was, from every point of view, unsatisfactory. It was rather a daring thing to no-ball Mold at Manchester, of all places in the world, but even Phillips' bitterest opponents must admit that since he took up this question of unfair bowling he has shown no lack of courage. Before he dealt with Mold last season at Nottingham he had no-balled Jones in Australia and Mr. C. B. Fry and Tyler in this country. We cannot pretend to be surprised at what occurred yesterday, as we have been told by competent eye-witnesses that Mold's delivery was open to grave objection, both in the Lancashire and Sussex match at Old Trafford last week, and in the Lancashire and Gloucestershire match at Gloucester on June 24. So far, indeed, from thinking Mold an ill-used man, we hold a strong opinion that he was very fortunate to be allowed to go unchecked through so many seasons. It is all very well for Mr. Hornby, Mr. Swire, and others interested in Lancashire cricket to say that Mold is a perfectly fair bowler, but the weight of expert opinion against them is overwhelming. At the captains' meeting at Lord's in December, Mr. MacLaren raised a direct issue by asking for a pronouncement on the point, and on a vote being taken eleven of the twelve cricketers present gave it as their deliberate opinion that Mold's delivery was unfair, MacLaren himself constituting the minority. Surely no condemnation could have been stronger than this.

However, we look at the question from a far wider standpoint than Mold's individual case, and we have no hesitation whatever in saying that the crusade against unfair bowling, undertaken first by Phillips, and followed up by other umpires, has been of immense benefit to cricket. We have not for over twenty years been so free from throwers in first-class matches as we are this season, and there can be no doubt in the minds of unprejudiced people that the improvement has been brought about, first by Phillips and his brother umpires, and secondly by the uncompromising attitude taken up by the captains at their meeting. The point nearly always overlooked when the question of throwing comes under discussion is that the evil caused by an unfair bowler is never limited to the culprit himself. A bad style passed as fair at Lord's, Manchester, or anywhere else, finds imitators, and the mischief spreads, like an infectious disease. In proof of this one has only to recall what was experienced years ago at

Uppingham School. The late H. H. Stephenson was one of the best of coaches, but he had very lax ideas on the subject of unfair bowling, and, as a natural result, Uppingham sent forth into the cricket world a batch of undoubted throwers. A well-known Uppingham cricketer, who for a season or two occupied a very prominent position, said to us once, 'I hope I bowl fairly; I always try to, but you know I came from a very bad school'.

In view of the forthcoming visit of English cricketers to Australia, we are not sorry that throwing has again become a burning question. In the Colonies things are by no means what they should be, there having for some time been a sad falling off from the standard of fair bowling that was once maintained. We saw clear proof of this during the tours of the Australian teams in this country in 1896 and two years ago. Such bowlers as Jones, McKibbin, and Noble would not have been tolerated in the elevens that came here between 1878 and 1890. Cricketers will remember that Spofforth went so far as to say in print that McKibbin's delivery was so bad that he ought never to have been allowed to bowl at all. Matters have certainly not improved lately, and last winter Marsh, the aboriginal bowler, who plays for New South Wales, was no-balled between a dozen and twenty times in one innings. Moreover, we learn that, in a letter received in London some little time back, a prominent member of Darling's eleven of 1899 said that one or two umpires like James Phillips were badly wanted in Australia, as all the young bowlers who had recently come to the front were more or less doubtful in their delivery. Here for the moment we may leave the question, merely adding that safety only lies in the rigid enforcement of the law. When once deliveries of doubtful fairness are permitted there is no telling where the trouble will end. As Phillips says, when a bowler strikes one at first sight as being a thrower the odds are a hundred to one that he is not bowling fairly.

Our Manchester Correspondent, telegraphing last night, says: The no-balling of Arthur Mold at Old Trafford to-day has caused great excitement in Lancashire cricketing circles. Since he was no-balled at Nottingham last year Mold has not bowled in any match in which Phillips has umpired, although Phillips on two previous occasions this summer has officiated in Lancashire matches. It was anticipated by the county committee that there might be interesting development, and, having full confidence in the fairness of Mold's delivery, they had given MacLaren instructions to put Mold on and have the matter thoroughly tested. The first over was bowled with Phillips standing at square-leg; Richardson, of Leicester, was the umpire at the bowler's end. That over passed unchallenged, but five balls were no-balled in the second over and three in the third. So the thing went on until eighteen no-balls were called of the ten overs, from three of which there were scores made. There was great excitement, the crowd jeering at Phillips. After ten overs Mold had a rest, but came on again just before lunch, and bowled three more overs, which were absolutely unchallenged. After lunch he bowled nine successive overs also unchallenged.

In the course of conversation later Richardson, the other umpire, declared that he was in as good a position as Phillips to judge every ball Mold bowled, and all, in his opinion, were perfectly fair. Mold was somewhat reluctant to talk of the matter, but, pressed on the subject, said he could not quite understand Phillips's action, especially as he allowed him to bowl twelve successive overs without no-balling him. He ought, so far as he knew—and his opinion was borne out by several players with whom he had conversed—never to have been challenged from first to last.

Mr. Swire, the hon. secretary, said that the committee had decided to have the matter settled one way or the other, believing that Mold was a perfectly fair bowler. He and Mr. Hornby watched the bowler's arm during the time Phillips was no-balling him, and they were not able to detect any suspicion of unfair bowling. Mr. H. G. Garnett declared most emphatically that there was neither rhyme nor reason in Phillips's action. He added that he (Mr. Garnett) played cricket purely for the love of the game, and that if he thought there was anything unfair in Mold's bowling he would not play.

Mr. A. C. MacLaren remarked that his opinion was pretty well known. He thought it was rather strange that Phillips stood alone among the English umpires in the attitude he had taken up. He felt more sorry for Mold than for anybody else, because it was a reflection upon a grand career, which might interfere with his subsequent cricket. As to the future, he assumed that other umpires would continue the attitude they had observed all the summer.

A. PAISH   Slow left-hand

Gloucestershire v. Nottinghamshire
Bristol. May 14, 15, 16, 1903

Gloucestershire v. Yorkshire
Bristol. May 18, 19, 1903

Paish was a slow left-hand bowler who, although suspect, had survived in the Gloucestershire team for some seasons. The match against Nottinghamshire was the first of the season and Paish was called by W. A. J. West. In the following match, against Yorkshire, West again officiated and called Paish four times. This ended Paish's career with Gloucestershire.

R. WHITEHEAD   Medium right-hand

Lancashire v. Nottinghamshire
Old Trafford. June 29, 30, July 1, 1908

Whitehead had a most remarkable début. He rescued his side with a brilliant innings of 131 not out, but on the same day was no-balled by Brown for throwing. The umpire objected to his fast ball, but expressed himself as satisfied with his normal delivery. Whitehead played for his county until the outbreak of the First World War without further interference.

G. JOHN   Fast right-hand

West Indian XI v. M.C.C.
Georgetown. February 27, 28, March 1, 1911

John was called more than once in M.C.C.'s first innings, but he later toured England with the West Indies in 1923 and passed without comment from any English umpire.

R. A. HALCOMBE   Fast right-hand

Western Australia v. Victoria
Melbourne. January, 1930

At this time Western Australia did not compete in the Sheffield Shield Competition, so this was a 'friendly' match. Halcombe bowled but one over, in the course of which he was no-balled six times by umpire A. N. Barlow.

E. GILBERT   **Fast right-hand**

Queensland v. Victoria
Melbourne. December 18, 19, 21, 22, 1931

Gilbert opened the Queensland bowling and when he was taken off after three overs he had taken one for 10—and been called eleven times. The umpire was A. N. Barlow.

H. J. COTTON   **Fast right-hand**

South Australia v. Victoria
Melbourne. November 13, 14, 16, 17, 1936

Cotton, an opening bowler, took over fifty wickets for South Australia in the Sheffield Shield, but this was the only occasion on which he was called—again by A. N. Barlow.

S. MOBARAK ALI   **Slow right-hand**

Trinidad v. Barbados
Bridgetown. July, 1942

Mobarak Ali was called as many as thirty times in a single innings. See text, page **26**.

R. R. FRANKISH   **Medium right-hand**

Western Australia v. Victoria
Melbourne. February 16, 17, 19, 20, 1951

Frankish bowled only four overs in the match (taking two wickets) and was called by umpire A. N. Barlow.

F. RIDGWAY   Fast-medium right-hand

M.C.C. v. Bahawalpur-Karachi
Bahawalpur. November 24, 25, 26, 1951

One of Ridgway's deliveries was called by the umpire at the bowler's end after Ridgway had deliberately thrown the ball.

M. R. REGE

Maharashtra v. M.C.C.
Poona. December 21, 22, 23, 1951

Rege was called twice by the bowler's umpire in the only over he bowled in the match.

C. N. McCARTHY   Fast right-hand

Cambridge University v. Worcestershire
Worcester. June 25, 26, 27, 1952

McCarthy had been suspected when touring with a South African team of 1951 and later whilst in residence at Cambridge University. This, however, was the only occasion on which he was officially challenged, by umpire P. Corrall.

G. A. R. LOCK   Slow-medium left-hand

Surrey v. Indians
The Oval. July 26, 28, 29, 1952

Lock was no-balled by umpire W. F. Price three times in the course of the match, twice in one over. This incident occurred very shortly after Lock's first appearance for England at Old Trafford against India. It was his fast ball which was challenged in each case.

G. A. R. LOCK   Slow-medium left-hand

England v. West Indies - First Test
Kingston, Jamaica. January 15, 16, 18, 19, 20, 21, 1954
M.C.C. v. Barbados
Bridgetown, Barbados. January 29, 30, February 1, 2, 3
1954

Lock was no-balled in the first of the above instances by umpire Perry Burke, who objected to his fast ball. In the second case, he was called by both umpires, H. Walcott and C. Jordan.

D. B. PEARSON   Fast right-hand

Worcestershire v. Gloucestershire
Bristol. June 30, July 1, 1954

Pearson's action had been adversely observed for some time. As a result of this set-back he took steps to alter the fault and was not again no-balled until 1959.

K. N. SLATER   Fast right-hand and medium off-spinner

Western Australia v. Victoria
Melbourne. November 8, 9, 11, 12, 1957

Slater was a versatile bowler who could bowl slow-medium off-breaks or fastish seamers. On this occasion he was bowling slow-medium pace. Later in his career Slater played for Western Australia and Australia against P. B. H. May's side in 1958–9.

C. STAYERS   Fast-medium right-hand

British Guiana v. Barbados
Bridgetown, Barbados. January, 1959

Stayers was a fast-medium bowler and, normally, of loose, somewhat gangling action. His fast ball or bouncer was in the opinion of
players and observers, who saw him in action against the M.C.C.
touring side of 1959–60, a definite throw.

G. M. GRIFFIN   Fast right-hand

Natal v. Transvaal
Durban. February 20, 21, 23, 1959

Griffin, who opened the bowling for Natal, was called for the first
time in his career, by umpire D. Fell. Griffin took two for 61 and
two for 19 in the match.

G. M. GRIFFIN   Fast right-hand

Natal v. Border and Eastern Province
East London. March 6, 7, 1959

This was an end-of-season trial match, Griffin bowling only eight
overs (for 18 runs) in the two innings. He was called by umpire A.
Kidson.

D. B. PEARSON   Fast right-hand

Worcestershire v. Indians
Worcester. April 29, 30, May 1, 1959

Pearson, having escaped censure since 1954, was no-balled five
times on the first day by J. S. Buller, himself a former Worcestershire
player. The home captain, D. Kenyon, persevered with Pearson
throughout the match, who, presumably, was able to modify his
delivery to pass the umpires' scrutiny as no further incident arose.

D. B. PEARSON   **Fast right-hand**

Worcestershire v. Essex
Worcester. May 16, 18, 1959

For the second time in successive home matches Pearson was no-balled, this time by umpire J. B. Bowes.

G. A. R. LOCK   **Slow-medium left-hand**

Surrey v. Glamorgan
Cardiff. July 8, 9, 10, 1959

Lock was twice no-balled by P. A. Gibb in Glamorgan's first innings. This was the only occasion upon which Lock was called during the season.

K. J. ALDRIDGE   **Fast-medium right-hand**

Worcestershire v. Leicestershire
Kidderminster. July 18, 20, 21, 1959

Aldridge had formerly played for Kidderminster. In a crowded hour before his fellow citizens he hit three sixes in one over, took three wickets for two runs in his opening spell, and was twice called for throwing by Buller. The seasonal report in *Wisden* states that both Aldridge and his clubmate Pearson 'did their best to rectify any fault'.

J. McLAUGHLIN

Queensland v. New South Wales
Sydney. January 1, 2, 4, 5, 1960

McLaughlin was primarily a batsman, who rarely bowled, so this case may be regarded as academic. On this occasion he was the seventh bowler to be tried, and given but a single over.

K. J. ALDRIDGE   Fast-medium right-hand

Worcestershire v. Glamorgan
Pontypridd. April 30, May 2, 3, 1960

Aldridge was no-balled by Crapp in Glamorgan's first innings. As Buller stood at the other end, Aldridge must have conformed at this warning, for he bowled unchecked in the second innings.

H. J. RHODES   Fast right-hand

Derbyshire v. South Africans
Derby. May 7, 9, 10, 1960

There had been certain misgivings about Rhodes' action since he had turned to fast bowling some years previously. This was the first time he was officially challenged, Gibb calling him six times during the South African innings in which he bowled thirty-one overs. It was the start of a protracted controversy which at the moment of writing remains largely unsettled. This action is complicated by the fact that Rhodes has an extension of the elbow joint, a matter discussed in the text, see pages **49–50** and **75**.

There was an ironical twist to this match in that Griffin, who bowled roughly the same number of overs, passed both umpires as regards his action, but was twice no-balled for dragging.

D. B. PEARSON   Fast right-hand

Worcestershire v. Northamptonshire
Dudley. May 21, 22, 23, 1960

Pearson was twice no-balled by Bartley in Northamptonshire's second innings. This was the last occasion upon which he was no-balled, as a serious decline in form ended his career the following season.

E. M. BRYANT   Slow left-hand

Somerset v. Gloucestershire
Bath. June 4, 6, 7, 1960

Bryant was no-balled five times by Yarnold on the first day of the match and did not bowl again. He only played two matches for his county thereafter and has not since reappeared.

G. M. GRIFFIN   Fast right-hand

South Africans v. M.C.C.
Lord's. May 21, 23, 24, 1960

This was the first occasion upon which Griffin was actually no-balled in this country and created a precedent in that he was the first visiting cricketer to England to be called for throwing. He was called once by Lee, and twice by Langridge.

G. M. GRIFFIN   Fast right-hand

South Africans v. Nottinghamshire
Trent Bridge. May 28, 30, 31, 1960

On this occasion Griffin, in the first innings, was called three times for throwing by Bartley and twice by Copson. He was also called three times in the second innings. As a result of these objections Griffin spent three days with Alf Gover in an endeavour to smooth out the bend and jerk in his action.

G. M. GRIFFIN   Fast right-hand

South Africans v. Hampshire
Southampton. June 18, 20, 21, 1960

Griffin enjoyed a period of immunity from the charge of throwing for a brief spell which included the first Test. It seemed that he had lost some pace in the process and possibly in trying to regain it he ran foul of umpires Parks and Harry Elliott at Southampton, where he was called six times.

G. M. GRIFFIN   Fast right-hand

South Africa v. England
Lord's. June 23, 24, 25, 27, 1960

Despite the doubts about his action Griffin was picked for the second Test match. He had an eventful opening two days, taking four wickets, doing the first hat-trick by a South African cricketer in a Test match, and being called eleven times by Lee for throwing. When his side were defeated by an innings he opened the bowling in the ensuing exhibition match and was immediately and persistently no-balled by Buller, being compelled to finish the over underhand. It was clear that this was the end of Griffin's career as a bowler.

D. W. WHITE   Fast right-hand

Sussex v. Hampshire
Hove. July 6, 7, 8, 1960

The umpires in this match were Gibb and Price, both known to be resolute in their opposition to illegal bowling. It was in fact Gibb who called White three times.

R. T. SIMPSON   Slow right-hand

Nottinghamshire v. Derbyshire
Trent Bridge. August 13, 15, 16, 1960

This may be regarded as a frivolous case. Simpson went on to bowl when Derby required five runs to win with nine wickets in hand, and playfully threw the last ball.

B. QUIGLEY   Medium-fast right-hand

South Australia v. Victoria
Adelaide. November 4, 5, 7, 1960

Quigley was twice called in Victoria's first innings by umpire Egar
from the bowler's end. He did not play for the State again.

B. K. BOSE   Slow right-hand
East Zone v. Pakistan
Jamshedpur. December 25, 26, 27, 1960

This was the seventh match of Pakistan's 1960–1 tour of India. Bose,
an experienced Ranji Trophy cricketer, was called three times in his
twenty overs and did not take a wicket.

H. J. RHODES   Fast right-hand

Derbyshire v. Northamptonshire
Derby. August 5, 7, 8, 1961

Rhodes, who had been the only bowler to be reported during the
'truce' earlier in the season, was thrice called for throwing by Gibb
in Northamptonshire's only innings. Carr, the Derbyshire captain,
took Rhodes off immediately and employed him at the other end
where Jepson raised no objection.

C. C. GRIFFITH   Fast right-hand

Barbados v. Indians
Bridgetown. March 16, 17, 19, 1962

It was in this match that the unhappy accident to N. J. Contractor
occurred when he was hit on the head by a ball from Griffith. Later
in the match umpire C. Jordan no-balled Griffith—the first call
against him in his career, and the only one until 1966.

I

I. MECKIFF   **Fast left-hand**

Victoria v. South Australia
Adelaide. January 11, 12, 14, 15, 1963

This was the first occasion in first-class cricket on which Meckiff was
no-balled for throwing. He was called early in South Australia's
first innings by umpire J. M. Kierse, but went on to finish with
eight wickets in the match without being called again.

I. MECKIFF   **Fast left-hand**

Victoria v. Queensland
Brisbane. March 1, 2, 4, 5, 1963

For the second time in the Sheffield Shield season of 1962–3 Meckiff
was called. He was no-balled in Queensland's second innings by
umpire W. Priem, though in all he bowled 38.3 overs in the match.

I. MECKIFF   **Fast left-hand**

Australia v. South Africa - First Test
Brisbane. December 6, 7, 9, 10, 11, 1963

This proved to be the culmination and the end of Meckiff's eventful
and bitterly controversial career. A return to form after a lean period
resulted in Meckiff's selection for the first match of the series. It was
known that Egar, one of Australia's leading umpires, had strong
views on illegal actions and it was generally realised that this would
be a crucial trial. Australia went into the field on the second day
and McKenzie bowled the first over. Meckiff then bowled with
Egar in the square-leg position. Egar allowed the first ball but called
the second, third, fifth and ninth. Meckiff was then taken off and
did not bowl again in the match, announcing his retirement soon
afterwards.

P. J. LAWRENCE   **Fast-medium right-hand**

Middlesex v. Sussex
Lord's. May 16, 18, 19, 1964

Lawrence, a young West Indian, was twice called by umpire Aspinall in Sussex's first innings. He conceded three runs in his three overs, and after this match—only his fourth in first-class cricket—he dropped out of the game.

I. R. REDPATH   **Medium-fast right-hand**

Australians v. Glamorgan
Cardiff. May 16, 18, 19, 1964

In the only over he delivered in the match Redpath was called by umpire John Langridge. Redpath was not a regular bowler and the incident had little significance.

E. ILLINGWORTH   **Fast-medium right-hand**

Victoria v. South Australia
Adelaide. November 13, 14, 16, 17, 1964

Illingworth was no-balled for throwing by both umpires, C. J. Egar and J. J. Ryan. He took four for 92 in thirty-one overs in South Australia's only innings. He was never a force in Victoria's attack and this was his only season in the State's first XI.

K. N. SLATER   **Fast right-hand and medium off-**
spinner

Western Australia v. New South Wales
Sydney. November 13, 14, 16, 17, 1964

For the second time in his Sheffield Shield career Slater was called. He was bowling off-spin, the offending ball being a faster one. The umpire was E. F. Wykes.

D. W. WHITE   Fast right-hand

Hampshire v. Lancashire
Old Trafford. June 9, 10, 11, 1965

'D. W. White, of Hampshire, was no-balled for throwing in an unusual incident in Lancashire's second innings at Old Trafford last
month. After stumbling in his run-up, he flung the ball—apparently
in a playful gesture—at D. M. Green, whereupon J. S. Buller
"called" him from square-leg. A no-ball was duly recorded in the
scorebook upon the instructions of the umpires.'
—*The Cricketer*, July 16, 1965

H. J. RHODES   Fast right-hand

Derbyshire v. South Africans
Chesterfield. June 26, 28, 29, 1965

Rhodes was called twice by Buller in the South Africans' second
innings. This intervention caused great resentment to a section of
the crowd, and Buller had to be protected by the police from angry
demonstrators. This match seemed to be ill-starred for Rhodes, who,
it will be recalled, was no-balled by Gibb in the same fixture in 1960.

R. COLLYMORE   Slow left-hand

British Guiana v. Jamaica
Kingston, Jamaica. February 26, 28, March 1, 2, 1966

Collymore was called five times for throwing by Douglas Sang Hue,
a vigilant umpire in these matters.

C. C. GRIFFITH   Fast right-hand

West Indians v. Lancashire
Old Trafford. May 18, 19, 20, 1966

Griffith was no-balled eight times for dragging over the line. He was also called for throwing by A. E. Fagg, but, curiously, this decision went unnoticed. It was not known to a vigilant press until the Lancashire players drew attention to it the following day. Originally it was thought that Fagg's call had coincided with a foot-fault called by Jakeman, but this was later proved to be untrue.

P. ROBERTS   Slow left-hand

Trinidad v. Jamaica
Kingston, Jamaica. February 8, 9, 10, 11, 1967

Roberts was called three times by Douglas Sang Hue in Jamaica's first innings. He finished the over but was then taken off.

D. ARCHER   Fast right-hand

Windward Islands v. Trinidad
Port of Spain, Trinidad. February 16, 17, 18, 1967

Archer was called in Trinidad's only innings, in which he bowled seven overs for 44 runs without taking a wicket. He did not play for Windward Islands again in the 1966–67 tournament.

(To end of English season of 1967)

John Nyren

Dedication of *The Young Cricketer's Tutor* to William Ward, Esq.

DEDICATION TO WILLIAM WARD, ESQ.

Dear Sir,

You have kindly consented to my wish of dedicating my little book to you, and I am much pleased that you have done so: first, because you are a countryman of my own—having lived in Hampshire; and secondly, and chiefly, because, as a CRICKETER, I consider you the most worthy man of the present day to reflect credit upon my choice as a patron.

It would ill become me, Sir, in this place to allude to other weighty reasons for congratulating myself upon this point—an insignificant book of instruction—as to the best mode of excelling in an elegant relaxation, not being the most fitting medium for digressing upon unquestionedly high public worth and integrity, or private condescension and amenity: at the same time, I cannot but feel how happily such a combination of qualities in a patron must redound to my own advantage.

I have not seen much of your playing—certainly not so much as I could have wished; but so far as my observation and judgment extend, I may confidentially pronounce you to be one of the safest players I remember to have seen. The circumstance of your rising so much above the ordinary standard in stature (your height, if I recollect, being six feet one inch), your extraordinary length of limb, your power and activity; to all which, I may add, your perfect judgment of all points in the game; have given you the superior advantages in play, and entitle you to the character I have given.

As a proof of its correctness, the simple fact will suffice of your having gained the 'longest hands' of any player upon record. This circumstance occurred upon the 24th and 25th of July, 1820, at Mary-le-bone, when the great number of 278 runs appeared against your name, 108 more than any player ever gained; and this, be it remembered, happened after the increase of the stumps in 1817.

May you long live, Sir, to foster and take your part in our favourite amusement; and may you never relax your endeavours to restore the game to the good old principles from which, I regret to say, it has in some instances departed since the time I used to be an active member of the fraternity. You are aware that I principally allude to the practice that the modern bowlers have introduced of throwing the ball, although in direct infringement of a law prohibiting that action.

I beg to subscribe myself,
Dear Sir,
Your faithful Countryman,
And obedient humble Servant,
JOHN NYREN.

Bromley, Middlesex
March, 1833.

John Nyren

Protest. From *The Young Cricketer's Tutor*, 1833.

PROTEST

AGAINST THE MODERN INNOVATION OF THROWING,

INSTEAD OF BOWLING THE BALLS

Having concluded my instructions to my young countrymen, before I finally take my leave of them, I feel anxious to place upon record my opinion respecting a new style of playing the game of Cricket which has been adopted only within these few years. As I have not been actively engaged in the field for several seasons, my motive for offering the following observations can arise solely from a wish to preclude the possibility that my favourite amusement, while it changes in feature, should deteriorate in character.

I conceive, then, that all the fine style of hitting, which the reader will find recorded in the latter part of this little work, must in a very material degree cease, if the modern innovation of throwing, instead of bowling the ball, be not discontinued. It is not the least important objection I have to offer against the system to say that it reduces the strikers too much to an equality; since the indifferent batsman possesses as fair a chance of success as the most refined player; and the reason of this is obvious, because, from the random manner of delivering the ball, it is impossible for the fine batsman to have time for that finesse and delicate management, which so peculiarly distinguished the elegant manoeuvring of the chief players who occupied the field about eight, ten, and more years ago. If the system continue, I freely confess that I cannot even hope again to witness such exquisite finish as distinguished the playing of such men as OLD

SMALL, and AYLWARD, and the TWO WALKERS, and BELDHAM, and LORD FREDERICK BEAUCLERC: the last indeed, I believe it is pretty well understood, retired as soon as the present system was tolerated.

I am aware that the defence which has been urged in behalf of the throwing, is, that 'it tends to shorten the game'; that now a match is commonly decided in one day which heretofore occupied three times the space in its completion. This argument I grant is not an irrational one; but if the object in countenancing the innovation, (and one, be it observed, in direct defiance of a standing law) extend solely to the 'curtailment of the game', why not multiply the difficulties in another direction? Why not give more room for display of skill in the batter? Why not have four stumps instead of three, and increase the length of the bails from eight inches to ten? The gentlemen forming the Mary-le-Bone Club have the power to order this. Will they consider the proposal, and sanction it, seeing that the fair character of their game is at stake? And that this is actually the case I feel perfectly confident, both from my own observation and experience, as well as from the corroboration of men, whose judgment I esteem. If, therefore, the present system be persisted in a few years longer, the elegant and scientific game of Cricket will decline into a mere exhibition of rough, coarse, horseplay.

I do not speak from prejudice, or from the partiality of one who has been educated in a particular school, however natural that such should be the result of my present opinion; but I can use my eyes, and I can compare notes and points in the two styles of playing; and they who have known me will bear testimony that I have never been accustomed to express myself rashly; I have, therefore, no hesitation in declaring that none of the players who have risen with the new system can compare for a moment in the standard of excellence (clever though they undoubtedly are) with the eminent men already named above, and for the reason I have assigned.

Bowling Actions. A Technical Analysis

The following article appeared in *The Cricketer Spring Annual* of 1960, under the heading of 'Bowling Actions' by Cricket 'Nompere'. It provides a pertinent study of the mechanics and ballistics involved in bowling, legitimate and otherwise.

Recent reports and opinions have drawn attention to the bowling of bumpers, their frequency and effect. A better understanding of the facts and figures underlying the actions of slow, medium and fast bowlers may assist club cricketers to appreciate certain aspects of speeds and directions of the ball at the moment it leaves the bowler's hand. Two opinions, relating to bumpers, are of importance. First, Sir Donald Bradman, on page 289 of his book, *Farewell to Cricket*, states that the bumper must be pitched so much shorter to make it lift. Second, Mr. A. R. Gover, on page 341 of the issue of THE CRICKETER dated July 19, 1958, states that to bowl the bumper the bowling arm must be pulled down at the moment of delivery and maximum speed must be obtained.

All this has prompted an examination of the subject of bowling actions with the object of ascertaining figures of speed and the direction of the ball which cricketers can realise and which can be the basis of experiments in the nets in the hope of improving their play. The ball, from the moment it leaves the bowler's hand up to the point of pitching, follows the geometrical form known as a parabola and, from the pitch until it reaches the batsman or goes beyond him, it also follows this form. The ball is, of course, subject to the well-known and easily understood scientific laws of motion. The figures now given are based on those laws.

A really fast bowler can bowl at 87 miles per hour and, with the pronounced dragging tendency of some such bowlers, the distance from the point at which the ball leaves his hand up to the striker receiving it can be only 18 yards. The first fundamental realisation of this in cricketers' minds should be that it takes only four-tenths of a second for a ball to travel this distance at such speed. Medical evidence, it is believed, indicates that it takes one-tenth of a second for the eye and mind to react to the conditions, leaving only three-tenths of a second or a little less for the proper playing of the stroke. In order to avoid injury to some strikers, umpires should be aware of this fact and, therefore, of the urgent necessity for dealing with all draggers to bring the front foot, it is suggested, back behind the popping crease and not allowing the bowler to drag his back foot through the bowling crease. Mr. Gover has indicated that the fast bowler must pull the ball downwards when bowling the bumper; in fact, it can be calculated quite easily that a fast bowler must impart a downward component of speed to each ball of his over at the moment of delivery; if he did not, every ball would be a full pitch.

At the other end of the range there is the slow bowler bowling at about 30 miles per hour. A good-length ball from a fast bowler will pitch about 15 feet or rather more away from the striker's wicket; for a slow bowler the good length will be about 11 ft. from this wicket, but these depend, of course, on the pace of the bowler and the pitch. In contradistinction to the fast bowler, the slow bowler must impart some upward speed to the ball as it leaves his hand to pitch on a good length. It is this initial upward path of the ball, or flighting by the slow bowler, which makes it difficult for a batsman to judge where the ball is likely to pitch. It is only as the ball starts to drop from the highest point of its path that the striker can assess its probable length with any accuracy.

In between the fast and slow bowler there is the medium-pace man. In his case it can be easily shown that if he imparts neither any upward nor downward component to the speed of the ball—that is, it leaves his hand in a momentarily horizontal direction—then, to pitch on a good length at 15 ft. from the striker's wicket, he must bowl at $52\frac{3}{4}$ miles per hour.

These considerations and the figures above now form some basis for computing initial upward or downward component speed figures and corresponding speeds at the point of pitching, also the height to which the ball may rise after pitching.

Using the ordinary equations of the laws of motion, it can be shown that a fast bowler must impart an initial downward speed of 11 ft. per second to pitch on a good length, but the slow bowler must give the ball an upward speed component of $14\frac{1}{2}$ ft. per second to pitch at 11 ft. from the striker's wicket. The slow ball would have to rise, at the top of its path, to a height of about $10\frac{1}{4}$ ft. above the ground, that is about $3\frac{1}{4}$ ft. above the level of the hand after it is released. The ball, on pitching from the fast bowler, will have a speed of 24 ft. per second as its vertical component, whereas the slow bowler will have a corresponding figure of $25\frac{3}{4}$ ft. per second. This explains what is commonly observed, that a ball from a slow bowler is apt to rise rather higher from a good length than from a fast or medium-pace bowler, because the ball hits the ground with a slightly higher vertical speed on account of the greater height from which it falls.

The fast bowler pitching shorter and shorter can make the ball rise higher because he has to impart a greater downward speed component to make the ball pitch shorter. If he pitches half-way up the pitch he must impart to the ball initially a downward portion of the speed of nearly 23 ft. per second, that is just over twice the figure for a good length ball and it will then hit the pitch at about $31\frac{1}{4}$ ft. per second as the vertical component of the speed. It will be seen that the shorter the pitching of the ball the higher the figure for the vertical speed component on pitching, in other words he is bowling bumpers, for he must slam the ball downwards into the ground with a speed of about 23 ft. per second as it leaves his hand. This merely proves by figures what has already been stated by Sir Donald Bradman and Mr. Gover.

The height to which the ball will rise after pitching is dependent on the depth of the pitch mark of the ball and the elasticity of the ground and ball. Taking the case of the medium-pace bowler it can be observed in play that the average height at which the ball hits or passes the wicket is about 2 ft. and that it will reach a maximum height of a little over $2\frac{3}{4}$ ft. beyond the wicket. This means that the good-length ball will have left the pitch with an upward speed of $13\frac{1}{2}$ feet per second after hitting the pitch at a downward speed of $21\frac{1}{4}$ ft. per second. What may be called a coefficient of rebound is then of the order of 0.6. The fast bowler will get more out of the pitch because the pitch mark will be deeper and the ball will tend to fly. If a figure for rebound is then taken as three-quarters, a fast bowler pitching half-way up the pitch will make the ball rise to a height of almost exactly 5 ft. at the striker's wicket, which agrees approximately with what can be observed on a field of play.

Naturally the question may arise in the mind of the susceptible batsman whether a fast bowler can impart an initial downward speed of virtually 23 ft. per second with a legitimate bowling action. This may not be beyond a tall fast bowler with a good wrist action but, in discussion, it has been said that some fast bowlers may (unwittingly it is sincerely hoped) appear to have a tendency at the last moment to throw some of their bumpers. Mr. Gover's view that the bowling arm must be pulled down at the moment of delivery might appear to lend support to an apparent throw, but would such an action come under the new definition of a throw? A bent arm at the instant of delivery following a straight bowling arm in the upward part of the bowling action could be described as a throw in reverse. Is this legitimate? A study of slow-motion pictures of the bowling action of various fast bowlers sending down bumpers would be very enlightening and, perhaps, enable a decision to be made.

Finally, the considerations discussed above may help in the understanding of fundamental facts underlying the bowling of bumpers. Of greater value will be the bowler's practical observation and personal analysis of results obtained by varying the factors of pitching length, height of the hand at the moment of delivery and the conscious imparting of an initial downward speed component at the moment of delivery. Such a bowler should be able to arrive at a better balanced practical result. Theoretical analysis cannot take into account practical factors such as hardness of the ground and locally varying conditions of texture of the pitch within a reasonable area of length pitching.

APPENDIX V

An Umpire's View

The following article appeared in *The Cricketer Spring Annual* of 1959, under the heading of 'Throwing—The Umpire's View' by Tom Smith, Hon. General Secretary of the Association of Cricket Umpires.

Even a possibility of the return of the throwing menace, with the attendant threat of unpleasant problems attached, will cause foreboding to all who participate in, and to all who love, cricket. Especially the umpires.

It is to be sincerely hoped that there will never be a return to that inglorious period of cricket, 1882–1902, when 20 stormy years were spent in endeavouring to find an answer to end the 'Throwing scandal'.

From 1882 onwards, umpires in this country were being exhorted to apply strictly the appropriate law to put a stop to something which was dangerous to the game. This was an impossible task. At this time the onus of 'calling' was on the bowler's end umpire. The impractibility of watching the bowler's feet and hand together, coupled with the variance of opinion of throwing definition, was too much.

Things went from bad to worse, and by 1896 throwing had found its stormy way to Australia. M.C.C. now followed with the granting to *either* umpire the power to call 'No ball' if not satisfied with the fairness of any delivery. Umpires—called into consultation—pinned the responsibility on to the county captains who, they claimed, should cease to select dubious players. Furthermore, umpires maintained, captains should stop their bowlers showing 'Flagrant dis-approval' on the field when called.

Before the 1901–2 season the county captains finally agreed not to play fourteen named bowlers, and the problem was completely and successfully solved.

During the ensuing fifty-seven years, throwing has, fortunately, become very rare. In 1959, however, the problem of something which is still as dangerous and detrimental to the game as ever, could rise again. History repeats itself, and many of the old questions are re-opened in the press and in discussion on radio and television.

Consider the difficulty of definition. There is, as there has always been, a heavy variation of general opinion. Umpires look for a straightening of the arm and elbow from the shoulder—an action quite different in itself from the body swing, and rotating arm from the shoulder. A bent elbow at the moment of delivery is *not* a throw, as is popularly thought. Neither, necessarily, is a flick of the wrist, and umpires do not take this action, alone, seriously. It can be argued, rightly, that it is impossible to throw without wrist movement, but many bowlers, endeavouring to get pace from the pitch, will use a legitimate wrist action. This wrist movement can be, quite in-correctly, defined as a jerk, and umpires have to be very careful indeed in forming a judgment.

Action seen by the camera can be very misleading, especially in slow motion, when angles of perspective and fore-shortening give exaggeration. It is important to watch for the straightening of arm and elbow from the shoulder, and essential to see an action 'live' before a fair decision can be given.

It will be seen that the umpire has an extremely difficult task in making an assessment as to what does, and does not, constitute a throw. A deduction and adjudication must be made from the result of reasoning based on his training and experience, as he sees the facts before him.

Apart from the unfairness, the insidious part of throwing is its infectiousness. One bowler seeing another getting away with it will himself try an occasional throw. Club cricketers tend to follow the patterns of changes in county cricket; young bowlers, particularly those at school, like to follow the example of what they see in senior cricket. This can lead to a serious degeneration in bowling, and decline in the game as a whole.

What are the solutions? Three are suggested, and are purely personal. The appropriate law states that if either umpire is not entirely satisfied with the fairness of a delivery the umpire shall call 'No ball'. In practice it is quite impossible for bowler's end umpire to watch the bowler's hand and feet together at the instant of delivery. It is at this moment of time that a decision must be reached. The umpire has as much as he can physically perform in concentrating on the bowler's feet, and immediate flicking of eyes to the pitch of the ball with follow-through for lbw, snicked catches, and so on. These things, and many others, happen in a split second. It is common sense, therefore, that the square-leg umpire should watch the bowler's hand. His colleague will concentrate on the feet position at the instant of delivery.

If a cricket match is to be efficiently and impartially umpired, it is absolutely essential that the two umpires should work together as a team. They must have complete confidence in each other, and assist and co-operate at every opportunity.

First Suggestion

Calling a bowler for throwing is a very unpleasant task. It is a serious matter for bowler and umpire. If square-leg umpire is worried by a bowler's delivery it would be better for him to consult his colleague for an opinion. Bowler's-end umpire could then move back a little and watch the bowler's arm at delivery. Both umpires are then in accord as to the fairness, or otherwise, of the delivery, and square-leg umpire can act with confidence, if necessary.

Second Suggestion

To avoid embarrassing field situations the two umpires, as soon as they are mutually agreed, would be empowered to approach the fielding captain—explain that they are dissatisfied with the bowler's action, and request that he be taken off. A joint report to club executives and parent body would follow. This would not eliminate the very occasionally thrown ball, but that would be dealt with on merit. The bowler would eventually come into the suspect category and be dealt with as above.

Third Suggestion

This is the old mixture as before, bringing an infallible cure. *Bowlers with suspect actions must not be allowed to bowl.* When in 1901–2 the county captains agreed that their fourteen named bowlers would not be played, they put an irrevocable end to throwing. This would be just as effective today. Linked with Suggestion 2, lists would be prepared from umpires' reports and action taken by the captains and club executives.

Umpiring is not easy, and nowadays umpires are coming more and more into the picture. In common with players, and humanity in general, they make an occasional mistake. At one time this was accepted as the 'rub of the green', but now it is not uncommon to find an umpire's decision given more prominence than the finest strokes, the best bowling or even match tactics.

That being so, the selection, knowledge and training of umpires for their difficult task is becoming more and more important. When consideration is given for dealing with throwing and other problems affecting the future of the game, it is essential that umpires be called into the councils.

K

Comment and correspondence from *The Cricketer* during the season of 1965

Rewriting the Throwing Law

From all the words spoken and written on the subject of throwing, one clear fact emerges—there is an urgent need to rewrite Law 26 to make its interpretation far easier than it is today.

If the Imperial Cricket Conference can make any progress in this direction at its meeting next month, it will have performed a major service. What is in issue is not just a quibble about laws, as some non-cricketers like to make out, but a matter which touches on players' personal safety. One hears of Australian batsmen breathing a sigh of relief at having come through the recent series in West Indies uninjured. Cricket is not a soft game but if this is to be the atmosphere in which it is played, it is surely not worth playing at all.

The wording of the experimental note to Law 26 reads at the moment: 'A ball shall be deemed to have been thrown if, in the opinion of either umpire, the bowling arm having been bent at the elbow . . . is suddenly straightened immediately prior to the instant of delivery.'

This is sensible enough on paper and probably adequate where the offender is a slow bowler. But it is no help to an umpire standing perhaps thirty yards away who has to make up his mind about an arm whirling over a bowler's head at speed. How can he be sure enough to take a step which may end a cricketer's career? Admittedly he can ask help from the camera, but even the film which that produces seems to be open to different interpretations according to the sympathies of the viewer. One school of support for Griffith in

West Indies admits that his arm straightens after having been bent but maintains that it is not *immediately prior* to the instant of delivery. What is 'immediately prior' and what is not? Who can say? The present law does not.

What form the new wording should take is something which should exercise the shrewdest brains among bowlers, coaches, umpires and administrators. But at least one suggestion offered seems to be worthy of serious discussion. This is that the only point to be considered is the straightness of the arm when held back horizontal before starting its final arc. If straight then, it is said, it cannot be bent into a throwing position before the moment of delivery.

Exhaustive examination of all types of bowler and action on film would be needed to determine whether this is always so. But it has one palpable merit, that the arm when behind the bowler is not only in clear silhouette but is usually slow moving and in some cases almost stationary.

Whether or not this proves to be a sound and helpful solution, remains to be discovered. But if a relatively simple definition can be found, it would do more than resolve the arguments and ill-feeling about throwing which are apt to crop up from time to time. It would make the periods of 'unawareness', such as occurred in the 1950's, less frequent. Any proposals made by M.C.C. about throwing since then, however genuine and valuable, have inevitably carried less weight because English cricket did not keep its own house in order in that period.

A simplification could have one other effect in a field, the importance of which was emphasised on this page recently. It would give a clear directive to coaches, so that young bowlers would be properly schooled and would not be allowed to progress to the higher grades of cricket with illegal methods likely to become a bitter embarrassment to them and many others.

FELIX

A Suggested Definition of Throwing

Sir,—It is lamentable that the International Cricket Conference which met recently at Lord's should, 'after long consideration', claim any degree of 'clarity' for their suggested 're-definition' of throwing. Indeed many would agree that, if this becomes law, it will make confusion worse confounded for our long suffering and despairing umpires, who will be even more apprehensive since the ruling has emanated from such an august body.

If the main object is to provide that the umpires shall have no possible, probable doubt whatever then the definition of a throw must be in terms quite simple and unambiguous. This, I contend, can never be achieved at a 'point immediately prior to the ball leaving the hand.'

In my long experience of bowling, and of watching other bowlers, there is clear evidence that most bowlers, as opposed to suspects, have their arms straight at a point in the final upward swing when the arm is horizontal with the shoulder. Surely, therefore, the rule might read: 'If in the opinion of either umpire the arm (or elbow) is bent after passing a point horizontal with the shoulder in process of delivery he shall call no-ball as the ball leaves the hand.'

This definition does not debar a bowler from using the wrist.

W. T. GRESWELL,
Orchard Combe, Weacombe, Bicknoller, Taunton.

We are pleased to publish the above letter from the President of Somerset, one of the best amateur bowlers of his generation. Mr. Greswell advocates precisely the suggestion made by Felix in THE CRICKETER *of June 4 in our leading article 'Rewriting the Throwing Law'.*—Editor.

A Definition of Throwing

Sir,—It was with great interest that I read the views of so eminent an authority as Mr. W. T. Greswell concerning the vexed problem of legislation on the question of throwing or, more correctly, legitimate bowling.

Being involved, in the role of a correspondent, in the controversy concerning Meckiff in Australia seven years ago I came to several definite conclusions at that time. I have not since then encountered any sufficiently convincing arguments to cause me to change my views.

The first necessity is for a clear ruling as to *why* a bowler infringes the law. Those who believe that 'anyone can tell a throw' have but to see the confusion and resentment aroused in perfectly honest minds when an umpire is bold enough to 'no-ball' a bowler on this assumption. The fierce controversies aroused by Meckiff and Rhodes are cases in point. It is most essential that 'justice be seen to be done'.

A definition to fulfil this need must be so simple and lucid as to be readily applicable on the spot and at the moment of infringement, without the paraphernalia of slow-motion cameras or such-like. It is the bowler's immediate action and not his reputation which is in question.

To describe a throw in such terms has so far proved impracticable and is, in all probability, impossible.

In 1958 I suggested that the definition of a bowl should be that 'when the arm reaches the horizontal, on the final swing, it shall be fully extended until the ball is released'. Mr. Greswell has expressed the identical requirement in different and possibly more precise terms. Either formula might or might not work in practice but I have yet to meet any persuasive argument as to why it might not.

The advantages as I see them are that an arm bent to the point where it is possible to throw the ball is clearly visible to all. The umpire is on the firm ground of fact, not 'opinion' or assumption, and so may act with a confidence at present denied him.

The objection that it would handicap the bowler who 'legitimately' bowls bent arm will not bear examination. He is, in my opinion, a rogue in any case, and his proscribement would be no loss. No great bowler has been *unable* to extend his arm. It is significant that sympathisers with this objection are prone to describe all the 'bent arms' that I can recall as 'chuckers'.

Having given this matter a great deal of thought over the years there are many further subtleties which space precludes me from advancing. But all point in the same direction; to the fact that so long as the bent arm is tolerated there will be recurrent confusion. On the other hand a generation strictly brought up under such a ruling as I have outlined would be entirely free of this form of pest.

IAN PEEBLES,
St. Mary Axe House, London, E.C.3.

Sir,—I am going to jump on the band-wagon with Bill Greswell and Ian Peebles because I agree wholeheartedly with their views on the subject of throwing as expressed in your columns.

I make one forecast, that firm and simple legislation will one day be introduced to solve what I consider the biggest blight on cricket since I have been connected with the game.

As Ian Peebles has said, his formula might or might not work in practice but I have yet to hear any good reason as to why it should not. I know that these views are shared by a number of cricketers from several different countries, many of whom are dismayed at the complicated interpretations upon which umpires have been asked to recognise a throw—and it is the unfortunate umpires who concern me most.

In conclusion, I share the view that the bent arm 'bowler' has no case for consideration, and his elimination would be in the best interests of all who conscientiously seek to observe the spirit as well as the letter of the law.

R. W. V. Robins,
Stafford Knight & Co. Ltd., Stevinson House, 155 Fenchurch
    Street, London, E.C.3.

The Job of the Umpires is Difficult

The Cricketer would be pleased to publish a letter from R. W. V. Robins on the vexed matter of throwing, if only because the time is surely over-ripe for the best and most experienced minds to ventilate their views on a subject which he describes as 'the biggest blight on cricket since I have been connected with the game'. (Most would say it ranked second to Bodyline in its evil implications, but that is by the way.)

It happens however that Mr. Robins' proposal accords perfectly with the suggestion, made by Felix in our leading article on June 4th, that it should be obligatory for the bowling arm to be fully extended at the horizontal and thereafter in the delivery swing. This was supported in a letter from W. T. Greswell, the President of Somerset, an admirable bowler in his day for his county and for Oxford, in *The Cricketer* of August 13th. Mr. Greswell's letter provoked one, published in our September issue, from Ian Peebles, whose opinion on the need for rewriting the Throwing Law has been consistent since the 1958–9 season when, touring Australia as a cricket writer, he saw various illegal actions in operation against P. B. H. May's team.

Mr. Robins' public accession to the ranks of those who favour a reform of the Law as proposed above is significant in that he has earned fame both as player, as captain of Middlesex and England, and as an administrator in several fields including Selection and Tour Managership.

Significant

Incidentally, like Mr. Peebles and Mr. Greswell, he was a bowler. No one could be better qualified to speak from experience. His views are also significant however in that until this issue he has considered himself debarred from writing on so controversial a subject by his membership of the Committee of M.C.C. It so happens that he retired from the Committee by rotation only at the end of September.

We believe that there are other excellently qualified men, including famous cricketers overseas, who favour what we may call 'the horizontal solution', but who are unwilling to announce their support for fear of committing their respective national bodies. They may indeed be debarred from doing so by the regulations of their Boards of Control.

The best justification for a law which stipulated that the arm must be fully extended (i.e. not bent at the elbow) from the horizontal position onward is that it would be easier of interpretation by the umpire. He would merely be required to adjudicate as to the straightness thenceforward of the elbow joint. Frankly, we believe that in a few cases such a rewriting of the law might need some revision of method by a few bowlers, chiefly off-spinners and orthodox slow left-arm spinners. Some of these in the effort to impart 'flight' are inclined either to flex the elbow slightly, or to bend it a little and keep it rigid. Such bowlers would need to limit their efforts at deception to variations in the speed of the arm and the use of the wrist (which, of course, can be manipulated with complete freedom).

Nothing to Fear

But the arms of ninety-nine bowlers out of a hundred are fully extended from the horizontal point onward, and that of the hundredth could be so extended with some small adjustment.

The legitimate bowler would have nothing to fear.

Our last point is not the least important. We believe that a further change in the law in the direction we have outlined, and the obliteration of the completely unhelpful amendment proposed by the International Cricket Conference in July, is imperative. But no rewriting of the law absolves the authorities of the game at all levels, from club through county or state to Test match, from responsibility for the actions (in all senses) of those whom they choose to wear their colours.

From every sort of personal consideration umpires have always been intensely reluctant to no-ball for throwing. Human nature does not change and probably they always will be. In any case the thrower, except for the most blatant, is far from easy to detect. What the horizontal solution would do, as we believe, is to make an extremely difficult job in this respect distinctly less so.

E.W.S.

The Position and the Answer

1. *The Law (Law 26)*

For a delivery to be fair the ball must be bowled, not thrown or jerked: if either umpire be not entirely satisfied of the absolute fairness of a delivery in this respect, he shall call and signal 'No ball' instantly upon delivery.

2. *Experimental version,* 1965

As an experiment in 1965 M.C.C. and the counties framed the following provisions (which, of course, contract out of the Law) for use in Tests and first-class matches:

For a delivery to be fair, the ball must be bowled not thrown: if, in the opinion of either umpire, a delivery is unfair in this respect, he shall call and signal 'No ball' instantly upon delivery. At the conclusion of every match, both umpires will submit reports to the Secretary of M.C.C., on the fairness or otherwise of the actions of all bowlers in the match. In the event of an umpire expressing doubt as to the absolute fairness of a bowler's action, the Secretary of M.C.C. shall inform the Secretary of the County Club, or the Manager of the Touring Team, concerned. The Captains may also report, if they have any doubt about the fairness of the action of any bowler in the match.

The following additional Note to be added to the Law:

A ball shall be deemed to have been thrown if, in the opinion of either umpire, the bowling arm, having been bent at the elbow, whether the wrist is backward of the elbow or not, is suddenly straightened immediately prior to the instant of delivery. The bowler shall nevertheless be at liberty to use the wrist freely in the delivery action.

3. *The suggested I.C.C. wording*

At the I.C.C. meeting at Lord's on July 15 it was suggested to Boards of the member countries that they adopt the following experimental wording:

A ball shall be deemed to have been thrown if, in the opinion of either umpire, the bowling arm is straightened, whether partially or completely, immediately prior to the ball leaving the hand.

4. *'The Horizontal Law'* (as proposed by Ian Peebles)

The ball shall be bowled, not thrown or jerked. That is to say that when, on the final swing, the bowler's arm reaches the horizontal it shall be fully extended from shoulder to wrist until the ball is released. This does not preclude the use of the wrist.

Sir,—It was with interest that I read Mr. Robins' letter published in your October issue. Among the many cricketers to whom he refers I am one who has entirely agreed with Mr. Peebles's definition of a fair delivery ever since he formulated it some years ago. It is logical, and, what is of paramount importance, it is reasonably easy to interpret. The experimental wording suggested at the I.C.C. meeting is difficult to interpret and does not take care of the fact that a ball can be thrown by bending the arm from the straight at the moment of delivery. I am certain that, in the interests of cricket and in fairness to umpires, the laws should be as logical and easy of interpretation as they possibly can be made.

The present lbw. law, dating from 1935, which permits a batsman to intercept with his front foot a ball which, if intercepted by his back foot, is out must be the most illogical law ever introduced into cricket. This law, particularly in this country where the ball deviates more, has, in my opinion, done untold harm to the game. Among its many evils it has decreased off-side play by putting a premium on in-swing and in-slant bowling. Modern bowlers, in order to take advantage of this and make the ball move in from the off side, are delivering the ball while the body is full-chested to the batsman. This, in my opinion, has contributed largely to the menace of throwing. Bowlers who deliver the ball sideways-on are not throwers. Bowlers with the actions of Larwood, Allen, McDonald and, in more recent years, Lindwall, Hall, etc., would, I contend, find it impossible to throw their delivery.

Cricket is a sideways game, as has always been demonstrated over the years by the greatest exponents, and this applies not only to bowling but to batting and, to some extent, to fielding.

If the majority of the present-day players would realise this, and put it into practice, I feel that a lot of the beauty of cricket, which I fear has been lost, would return.

R. E. S. WYATT,
The Old Forge, Wimpstone, nr. Stratford-on-Avon.

Sir,—I am happy to support *The Cricketer* solution forbidding the arm to be bent after the horizontal. It seems to me that in the last resort the umpire must be the judge no matter how long one sits in committee and no matter how many photographs of varying kinds are put forward. In view of this one must produce an answer which can be easily and simply interpreted by the umpire and your suggestion, as I see it, is the best and simplest I have read or heard.

J. C. LAKER,
2 Princes Street, London, W.1.

Sir,—May I come out in support of Ian Peebles's proposed 'Horizontal Law', the simple solution to a cricket law which so far has eluded a wording which would be fair to both umpire and player alike.

If the 'Horizontal Law' was adopted it would surely simplify the umpires' job, and unanimity of opinion on a player's action would then become the common order instead of the disagreement we saw from our umpires last season.

The 'photo-finish' which seems to be at the end of so many of our assessments of a bowler's action would no longer be necessary if the majority of umpiring verdicts were against him. The unfortunate player, too, would be prepared to bow to a majority decision.

I have been asked to help suspect bowlers several times in the past few years and had the Peebles 'Horizontal Law' been in effect, the 'cure', from both the pupil's point of view and my own, as coach, would have been simplified.

On the other hand, the 'Horizontal Law' would work against those who are suspect at the present time. As I see it, there are two different methods used. One is to bend the bowling arm at shoulder level so that the elbow points outwards and the knuckles of the hand are towards the side of the face. The other is to keep the arm bent from the elbow throughout the action. It is almost a physical impossibility to straighten the arm at the moment of release, using these two methods.

These bowlers would have to alter their technique radically because under the Peebles idea they would be blatant breakers of the law.

Ian Peebles has gone back to the simple form which worked in the earlier days of the game. Throw with a bent arm, bowl with a straight arm.

A. R. GOVER,
Gover Cricket School, London, S.W.18.